Feasting on the Word

OTHER BOOKS BY THE AUTHOR

Feasting on the Word

J. Vernon McGee

THOMAS NELSON PUBLISHERS
Nashville

Published in Nashville, Tennessee, by Thomas Nelson, Inc., and distrib-
uted in Canada by Lawson Falle, Ltd., Cambridge, Ontario.

Unless otherwise noted, Scripture quotations are from the KING JAMES
VERSION of the Bible.

Scripture quotations noted NKJV are from the NEW KING JAMES VER-
SION of the Bible. Copyright © 1979, 1980, 1982, Thomas Nelson, Inc.,
Publishers.

Scripture quotations noted Scofield are from the Scofield Study Bible.
Copyright © 1967, Oxford University Press, Inc., New York.

Library of Congress Cataloging-in-Publication Data

McGee, J. Vernon (John Vernon), 1904–1988
   Feasting on the word / J. Vernon McGee.
      p.   cm.
   ISBN 0-8407-7680-2 (hard)
   1. Sermons, American.   I. Title.
BV4253.M365   1992
252—dc20   92-24543
                                                       CIP

Table of Contents

1. The Human Story (Genesis 3) — 1
2. King Solomon and the Queen of Sheba — 15
   (1 Kings 10:24; 2 Chronicles 9:3–4)
3. An X-Ray of the Cross (Psalm 22) — 29
4. World Dominion: Whose Will It Be? (The Times — 43
   of the Gentiles) (Daniel 2)
5. When God Became Man (John 1:1–18) — 63
6. He Is Coming Again! (John 14:3) — 81
7. Behind the Black Curtain in the Upper Room — 95
   (John 13:33–14:27)
8. Living the Christian Life—God's Way — 109
   (Romans 8:1–23)
9. Walking in the Spirit (Galatians 5:16) — 127
10. Charge It (The Epistle to Philemon) — 139
11. Why Do God's Children Suffer? (Hebrews 12:3–15) — 155
12. Three Worlds in One (2 Peter 3) — 183
13. What Can Believers Do in Days of Apostasy? — 223
    (The Epistle of Jude)
14. The Pulpit and the Well of Life (John 12:21) — 243

1

THE HUMAN STORY

(Genesis 3)

There is a question which every thinking mind has asked. You have asked it. It has even invaded the field of nursery rhyme as found in George MacDonald's poem:

> *Where did you come from, baby dear?*
> *Out of the everywhere into the here.*

"Whence came man?" has been the common question down through the ages, and it demands an answer. The statement of reply given in this little rhyme is neither scripturally nor biologically accurate, but it faces the problem of origin.

Where did the human race begin? What is the origin of man? Many explanations have been offered. Some have been popular for awhile and then discarded as lacking evidence. When I was sixteen years old I read Darwin's *Origin of Species* and then his *Origin of Man*. But Darwinian evolution is discredited today.

Dr. Arnold Brass made a tremendously revealing statement in his little pamphlet concerning Dr. Haeckel, an evolutionist. He said that Dr. Haeckel published forgeries in his book to prove his theory. Dr. Haeckel, admitting he had done that, replied saying,

> I should feel utterly condemned and humiliated by the admission were it not that hundreds of the best observers and most

1

reputable biologists lie under the same charge. The great majority of all morphological, anatomical, historical, and embryological diagrams are not true to nature, but are more or less doctored, systematized, and reconstructed.

And it was Dr. Watson, the great English evolutionist, who made the statement, "Evolution is a theory universally accepted, not because it could be proven to be true, but because the only alternative—special creation—was clearly incredible."

One of the reasons, I suppose, for the acceptance of evolution by so many is that it offers an "out" for man so that he does not have to accept the biblical account of creation. Without evolution man today is on the horns of a dilemma and has no theory. One agnostic recently declared, "We do not have to offer an explanation for the origin of man." In spite of his statement, man's mind cries out and wants a reply to the question, "Whence came man?"

THE ACT OF CREATION

For more than three thousand years Scripture has presented a written record of the origin of man. At first it had to overcome the superstition and idolatry of bygone days, and today it withstands the speculation of this agnostic, scientific age. The biblical account is couched in noble terms; it is written in lofty language. The latest findings, when laid parallel with the Genesis account, give cause for singing the Hallelujah Chorus. How majestic Genesis reads in our day!

As important as man is in our thinking, the Bible does not open with the story of his creation. It opens with the fact of God; He is the One who is preeminent in this Book. Should the whole world turn to atheism it would not alter the fact that there is a God and that He created all things.

God's first act of creation was to bring into existence the heavens and the earth. One summer I had the privilege of listening to Mr. Chestnut, a wonderful Christian layman who at that time headed up General Electric's Department of Research. He told us that it has been demonstrated in the laboratory that matter can be created out of energy. This is a more difficult process than that of breaking down the atom, but it has been accomplished. Having told us this, Mr. Chestnut then cited this profound passage from God's Word:

Through faith we understand that the worlds were framed by the word of God, so that things which are seen were not made of things which do appear. (Hebrews 11:3)

In other words, energy and power have been translated into matter. The Word of God is "living and powerful." God spoke and energy was translated into matter. This fact we have understood by faith. Today it is demonstrated in the laboratory.

Let us get another thing clear in our thinking. Genesis was not written as a scientific statement. Does that surprise you? I thank God that it was not, and here is my reason for that statement: It will compare with present-day scientific statements, but science is a changing subject, and if Genesis were written in the science of the hour it would be wrong twenty years from today. The nebular hypothesis of the French astronomer Pierre Laplace was good science a hundred years ago, but it is now discarded. Man changes his theories as he progresses in searching. No, the Genesis record is a *religious* record, and we should learn to compare it with the cosmogonies of that day.

Does the Genesis record contain scientific error? Constantly we hear the accusation that it does. A few years ago we were told that it would not stand, for it mentions light on the first day and does not mention the sun, moon, or stars until the fourth day and that light cannot be had without light-holders. But Genesis was accurate in those days of scientific attack, for we now know that there was light before there were light-holders, for cosmic light is a light that needs no light-holder. So the Genesis account stands.

> *In the beginning God created the heaven and the earth.*
> (Genesis 1:1)

I hold the view that following God's creative act a great catastrophe occurred—earth *became* without form and void. A curtain went down on the pre-Adamic creation, an iron curtain. There was, and is, no penetration of that curtain, and anything man says is pure speculation. You can put behind that curtain all the ages you may care to for this earth, but never forget that you are dealing with a God of eternity, and this little earth on which we live may have been here a long time—perhaps millions, billions, or terms of years known only in the language of eternity. Our God of eternity is not crowded for time. He has eternity behind Him, He has eternity before Him—and what are a few billions of years in His economy?

THE RECORD OF MAN

What many consider six days of creation in Genesis 1, I believe to be *renovation*, preparatory for a new tenant arriving. When man is created, and we are vitally concerned with him, this little earth becomes the center of interest in the universe so far as the Bible record is concerned. Formerly it was uranic—pertaining to the heavens; then the record changes to the geocentric—pertaining to the earth as the center. The telescope has been laid aside and now the microscope comes into use. No longer is it the study of the macrocosm—the universe, but the microcosm—man, human nature.

Here is the record that is given:

These are the generations of the heavens and of the earth when they were created, in the day that the LORD God made the earth and the heavens. (Genesis 2:4)

Now I have discovered that each time I read the Scriptures I find something new. It has been embarrassing for me to find something new in so familiar a chapter as this, but this I have done. Notice how it reads, "These are the generations of the heavens and of the earth. . . ." The heavens are mentioned first. Then when He begins to talk about man it reads: "In the day that the LORD God made the earth and the heavens." There is a right about-face; the earth becomes the center of interest because man is to be created and put on this earth.

Now here we note a word, the use of which is peculiar to Genesis. It is the word *generations,* and every time it is used it always gives the generations that are to follow, and the generations of the heavens and the earth are the generations of man. Now notice something that is quite wonderful, and keep in mind that when He speaks of the generations of the earth He is not speaking of what has preceded, but of what follows—He speaks of results and not causes; it is a superscription not a subscription—and the creation of man follows. Will you notice it:

And the LORD God formed man of the dust of the ground, and breathed into his nostrils the breath of life; and man became a living soul. (Genesis 2:7)

Man is at once the offspring of heaven and earth. These are the generations of the heavens and the earth, and now God takes dust—man is of the earth and earthy—but God breathes into his nostrils the breath of life. Man is not only of the earth, but man is of heaven. In fact, three stages are given here of creation:

(1) The creation of the world of matter:

> *In the beginning God created the heaven and the earth.*
> (Genesis 1:1)

(2) The creation of life:

> *And God created great whales, and every living crea-*
> *ture that moveth, which the waters brought forth abun-*
> *dantly, after their kind, and every winged fowl after his*
> *kind: and God saw that it was good.* (Genesis 1:21)

(3) The creation of man with spiritual capacities:

> *So God created man in his own image, in the image of*
> *God created he him; male and female created he them.*
> (Genesis 1:27)

These three phases find their conclusion in Paul's great statement: ". . . *your whole spirit and soul and body be pre-served blameless unto the coming of our Lord Jesus Christ*" (1 Thessalonians 5:23).

On the physical plane man is similar to the animal world. Now, just because a Ford automobile has four wheels, two headlights, and one steering wheel does not mean that it was made in the same factory as a Chevrolet. They are different though they both have the same basic parts. They are made this way because they are both going to operate on the same place, the highway. Man has two eyes, he has two ears, and he has a mouth, as also does the animal world, because both live in the same environment. This does not prove that one evolved from the other but that on the physical side man was made of dust, as the Scripture says. On the psychological side he has a soul, the functional part of man with his drives and his urges—which are too often depraved and perverted.

Then there is his spiritual side which came from God when God breathed into him the spirit of life. Man has a humble origin, and he has a high origin. He is both earthy and heavenly. God created out of dust one in His own image, and we are told that He remembers that we are dust. Too often we forget this. The psalmist said, "I am fearfully and wonderfully made."

Man the creature was made a free, moral agent. He was given the right of choice between good and evil, which is essential to personality; otherwise he would be an automaton. Having been given this right of choice he was put to the test, not to prove he could commit a crime, but rather to test his obedience to God. And here we find that when the devil tempted man, instead of resisting, he listened. God could have made man an automaton, but He did not. So man was able to break from this divinely arranged fellowship. Man doubted God, denied His Word and disobeyed Him. Disaster came and man became depraved.

Genesis 3 is the most important chapter in the Bible in explaining the tragic fruits of disobedience, from the Garden of Eden through the centuries of man's march to the present hour. This chapter draws a clear picture of the life of the town in which you live. In Genesis 1 and 2, you see man created and placed in the Garden of Eden. Now read chapter 3 which delineates our modern life, and you cannot but conclude that man is not in the Garden. Something tragic has happened—man disobeyed God. If you want to know how great was that disobedience and how tragic the results, listen to the Apostle Paul as he looked at the human story, and said:

> *Because that, when they knew God, they glorified him not as God, neither were thankful; but became vain in their imaginations, and their foolish heart was dark-*

ened. Professing themselves to be wise, they became fools, and changed the glory of the uncorruptible God into an image made like to corruptible man, and to birds, and fourfooted beasts, and creeping things. Wherefore God also gave them up to uncleanness. . . .
(Romans 1:21–24)

If you will look around you in your town today, you will see that uncleanness in countless thousands of lives.

An illustration of this comes from our own American Indians. Mr. Theodore Epp, who founded the "Back to the Bible" radio broadcast, told me that his father was one of the first missionaries to the Hopi tribe. He said that the missionary work was so unsuccessful at first that the Mennonite folk thought they would leave the mission, but Mr. Epp's father said, "I will go on with it. I will remain here." God rewarded his faith when one of the chiefs of the Hopi tribe was converted. This gave the first avenue of approach, and he could at least read the Bible to the Indians that gathered there.

One day he read in their hearing the first chapter of Romans. After the reading was over, one member of the council took him aside and angrily said, "Don't try to deceive us by saying that you got that out of the Bible. The chief has become a Christian and has told you about us, and you are telling us off by reciting our sins to us." This Indian was amazed to discover that this record had been written of mankind almost two thousand years ago by the apostle Paul. My friend, when man fell, his disobedience plunged an entire race into sin.

And when man's tragic fall took place it was flashed to the far corners of the universe. God's created intelligences read the headlines and mourned for little man who had lifted his midget fist in heaven's face and had defied God.

THE JUDGMENT OF MANKIND

As the result of his sin, a fourfold judgment came upon mankind. There was first of all a judgment upon the serpent.

And the LORD God said unto the serpent, Because thou hast done this, thou art cursed above all cattle, and above every beast of the field; upon thy belly shalt thou go, and dust shalt thou eat all the days of thy life. (Genesis 3:14)

Upon the animal world about us is this judgment of God. Paul, writing of it in the eighth chapter of Romans, says,

For the earnest expectation of the creature waiteth for the manifestation of the sons of God. For the creature was made subject to vanity, not willingly. . . . (Romans 8:19–20)

Now while there is this judgment resting upon the serpent, beyond the serpent there was another one—Satan, and we read that there was a judgment to come upon him:

And the great dragon was cast out, that old serpent, called the Devil, and Satan, which deceiveth the whole world: he was cast out into the earth, and his angels were cast out with him. (Revelation 12:9)

And still another judgment was pronounced—this was upon woman. God said that in sorrow she would bring forth children, but He also said:

And I will put enmity between thee [the serpent] *and the woman, and between thy seed and her seed; it shall bruise thy head, and thou shalt bruise his heel.* (Genesis 3:15)

Beloved, go to Bethlehem and look at the event that transpired there about two thousand years ago. That is God's work, not man's:

> *Behold, a virgin shall be with child, and shall bring forth a son, and they shall call his name Emmanuel, which being interpreted is, God with us.* (Matthew 1:23)

Now go to Golgotha and see the bruising of the woman's Seed. That is God's work, not man's. There was a transaction between God the Father and God the Son when He bore the penalty for the sins of the whole world. Yes, judgment came upon woman and upon this earth, and today the whole creation is travailing in pain, waiting for a deliverance that is coming through the redemption that is in Christ.

Then we find that a fourth judgment came, and it was upon man. Listen as God speaks to man:

> *In the sweat of thy face shalt thou eat bread, till thou return unto the ground; for out of it wast thou taken: for dust thou art, and unto dust shalt thou return.* (Genesis 3:19)

Whether we consider man laboring with a crude implement of the Stone Age or see him laboring under the tensions and pressures of this push-button civilization, it is still true that it is by the sweat of his face that he eats bread. It is God's judgment upon man.

This then is the human story. It is a sad story—the sob of the city and the sigh of the countryside. We find life filled with irritations, annoyances, disappointments, and resentments. Men's hearts are filled with frustrations, tensions, and complexes which can often lead a person to some high bridge or building and the plunge to death. It is a story of broken homes, hungry children, and neglected old people. The lullaby of Broadway is a theme in which the drunkard, the harlot, and the thief weave their way into the stream of honest folk. The light of liberty is gone out. Bitterness and wrath are in the hearts of men; envy and hatred are among nations, and strife and gossip are in the house of God. Such is the human story. Scripture says:

> *For men shall be lovers of their own selves, covetous, boasters, proud, blasphemers, disobedient to parents, unthankful, unholy, without natural affection, truce-breakers, false accusers, incontinent, fierce, despisers of those that are good, traitors, heady, highminded, lovers of pleasures more than lovers of God; having a form of godliness, but denying the power thereof. . . .*
> (2 Timothy 3:2–5)

But that, thank God, is not the final chapter. It is true that "by one man sin entered into the world, and death by sin," but it is also true that *"as by the offence of one judgment came upon all men to condemnation, even so by the righteousness of one the free gift came upon all men unto justification of life"* (Romans 5:18).

Today there stands a cross between us and the Garden of Eden. That cross is not an ambulance sent to a wreck! The Lord Jesus Christ is the Lamb of God slain before the foundation of the world. The cross is not God's second best; it is His very best. God closes the record of man's fall with this verse:

> *So he drove out the man; and he placed at the east of the garden of Eden Cherubims, and a flaming sword which turned every way, to keep the way of the tree of life.*
> (Genesis 3:24)

The cherubim were not to block the way, but God was saying in effect, "In spite of man's sin, I will keep the way of life open for him."

For God so loved the world, that he gave his only begotten Son, that whosoever believeth in him should not perish, but have everlasting life. (John 3:16)

And before the curtain goes down on man's little day, God lets us hear the strains of the finale, a mighty crescendo of praise—

And they sung a new song, saying . . . Thou wast slain, and hast redeemed us to God by thy blood out of every kindred, and tongue, and people, and nation; and hast made us unto our God kings and priests: and we shall reign on the earth. (Revelation 5:9–10)

Now listen to God's assurance found in Romans 8. Although guilt came upon man, today

who shall lay any thing to the charge of God's elect? It is God that justifieth. Who is he that condemneth? It is Christ that died, yea rather, that is risen again, who is even at the right hand of God, who also maketh intercession for us. (Romans 8:33–34)

There is now no condemnation to them which are in Christ Jesus—because Jesus died, arose from the dead, and today is at the right hand of God where He ever lives to make intercession for us. Paul asks the question, "Who shall separate us from the love of Christ?" Back in the Garden of Eden man was separated from God. But now we have the comfort and security of knowing that nothing can separate us from His love.

For I am persuaded that neither death, nor life, nor angels, nor principalities, nor powers, nor things present, nor things to come, nor height, nor depth, nor any other creature shall be able to separate us from the love of God which is in Christ Jesus our Lord. (Romans 8:38–39)

Today we have gained more in Christ than we lost in Adam, and I would rather be in the midst of this perverse civilization with Christ than in the Garden of Eden without Him. In Christ we have hope, salvation, deliverance, and security!

— 2 —

KING SOLOMON AND THE QUEEN OF SHEBA

(1 Kings 10:24; 2 Chronicles 9:3–4)

And all the earth consulted Solomon, to hear his wisdom, which God had put in his heart (1 Kings 10:24).*

The more I read this verse the more it impresses me. I am confident that God wants us to pause a moment and look at the significance of it. "All the earth consulted Solomon, to hear his wisdom." You see, God called the people of Israel to be His witnesses, but to be His witnesses in a different way from what He has called us to be. You recall that He has called us to go into all the world. Just prior to the day of pentecost, Christ told believers to begin at Jerusalem and to go out to Judaea, Samaria, and to the uttermost part of the earth (Acts 1:8). There was to be a moving away from Jerusalem.

---

* Bible quotations are from *The New Scofield Reference Bible.*

15

Today the witness of the church is always outward. We must face out if we are to be witnesses for Him. But that was not Israel's case. Israel was never called to go to any nation outside and witness; Israelites were not called to go as missionaries.

I have always had great sympathy for Jonah because God asked him to do something that He had not asked His people to do in that day. He asked Jonah to go to Nineveh. That was unusual. This exception to the rule was made because God wanted to save that great city, and He wanted to give them this opportunity. However, the method in that day was this: when the nation Israel was faithful and true to God, worshiping and obeying God in Jerusalem, it would be such a witness that the world would come to Jerusalem and would accept the invitation of Israel, which was, "O come, let us go up to Jerusalem to worship the Lord." The nations of the world would accept that invitation and would come. Did they ever do it? Was the nation Israel ever faithful to God in this respect?

It certainly was.

There was a brief period during the reigns of David and Solomon, which is approximately eighty years, almost a century, in which the word went out. During the reign of Solomon, we are told that all the earth heard, and that is not an exaggerated statement. All the civilized world, every great nation of that day, heard of the wisdom of Solomon, heard of the greatness of Solomon, and came to Jerusalem. Multitudes came to a saving knowledge of God because of that.

THE QUEEN OF SHEBA

Now the incident of the visit of the Queen of Sheba is given to us. She was one of the many who visited Solomon, and her visit is recorded while others are omitted for very definite reasons, I believe. One reason for its being recorded is that she came farther than anyone else. We are told she came from the ends of the earth, and that means the ends of the civilized world. She came over the only road, the only camel trail that led to Jerusalem; she came from way out yonder. Also her visit was rather unusual because she was a queen and because of the wealth of her kingdom.

The question has always been: from where did she actually come? Two places by the name of Sheba are known to us. One is in Africa and is the country known as Ethiopia. The other is on the Arabian peninsula and is the little country we know today as Yemen, that little country which has been left out of the oil situation and is so poor right now. Was the Queen of Sheba queen of Yemen or was she queen of Ethiopia? Bible expositors and scholars are divided on this. The queen of Yemen was known as the queen of the south, and the Lord Jesus Himself, you remember, spoke of the Queen of Sheba as the queen of the south (Matthew 12:42). Also Yemen was known as the country of spices in the ancient world, and spices seem to be the noteworthy gift which the Queen of Sheba brought to Solomon. It is interesting that both countries have the tradition that in ancient times their queen visited Solomon. Could there have been another queen who visited Solomon? I have a notion that there could have been a visit of another which was not recorded, since we are told that "all the earth consulted Solomon."

The important thing, as far as we are concerned, is that she came from the uttermost parts of the earth and that she came to visit this man Solomon.

Now I want you to notice something at this particular point. Israel was giving a testimony that God said she should give. At the time of the dedication of the temple here is the thing that is said concerning it:

Moreover, concerning the foreigner, who is not of thy people, Israel, but is come from a far country for thine great name's sake, and thy mighty hand, and thy out-

stretched arm; if they come and pray in this house, then hear thou from the heavens, even from thy dwelling place, and do according to all that the foreigner calleth to thee for, that all people of the earth may know thy name, and fear thee, as doth thy people, Israel, and may know that this house, which I have built, is called by thy name. (2 Chronicles 6:32–33)

This may seem strange to you, but the temple that Solomon built was not built for the nation Israel alone. It was built for the world. It was built that all nations might come to Jerusalem and worship. One of the saddest things they did was to make divisions in it. In the days of the Lord Jesus you find there is a court of the Gentiles and there's a court for the women—a court for this group and that group. God never intended that there be this segregation. All were to come to Him on the same plane and basis. This is the thing to which Paul called the attention of his people that made the church different from the temple. Speaking of Christ, he said:

For he is our peace, who hath made both one, and hath broken down the middle wall of partition between us, having abolished in his flesh the enmity, even the law of commandments contained in ordinances, to make in himself of two one new man, so making peace. (Ephesians 2:14–15)

Christ Jesus broke down the middle wall of partition between Jew and Gentile, between male and female, between rich and poor. All stand together on one plane before Him. Now, my beloved, that is something Israel should have done, that was the purpose of the temple; that was the reason it was built.

THE CALL TO COME

Now I want to turn to another passage of Scripture that records this dedicatory prayer of Solomon's.

> *Moreover, concerning a foreigner, who is not of thy people, Israel, but cometh out of a far country for thy name's sake (for they shall hear of thy great name, and of thy strong hand, and of thine outstretched arm), when he shall come and pray toward this house, hear thou in heaven, thy dwelling place, and do according to all that the foreigner calleth to thee for, that all people of the earth may know thy name, to fear thee, as do thy people Israel; and that they may know that this house, which I have built, is called by thy name.* (1 Kings 8:41–43)

Solomon is emphasizing, you see, at the dedication of the temple, that it is a temple for everyone. It was a place where every person on earth could approach the living and the true God.

That word went out; it went out to the ends of the earth in that day, and it reached the Queen of Sheba. Returning now to the record of the Queen of Sheba's visit, it begins with the words, "And when the queen of Sheba heard" (1 Kings 10:1). That's all. She first had to hear.

"So, then, faith cometh by hearing, and hearing by the word of God" (Romans 10:17). The gospel is something that you have to hear, and then you have to make your decision on whether or not you believe God. Faith comes by hearing the Word of God. This entire incident opens up out yonder at the ends of the earth with a queen who heard. Then she acted on what she heard.

My friend, that is the place where God will meet you, the only place He will meet you. You have to hear. I feel that my responsibility is to get the Word to that little ear gate. When I get it to your ear gate, my responsibility is over. From there on it is your responsibility, and God puts something between the two ears so you can make a decision relative to Him. The responsibility of all of us who are believers is to get God's Word to the ear gate of our neighbor, and when we have done that, we have done the thing God has called us to do.

Now at the time the Queen of Sheba arrived in Jerusalem, it was one of the most interesting cities in the world. There is not a city on earth today that is as thrilling to visit as Jerusalem was at that time. The "Graylines" had a tour that would take you everywhere in that day, and it would take more than a day to see everything that they had to show. Jerusalem was very interesting and was a tourist attraction.

When this queen arrived, I think she attracted a great deal of attention: she *had* to be unusual to attract attention. Centuries later wise men came out of the East because a greater than Solomon was there. They came with the question, "Where is He that is born king of the Jews?" (Matthew 2:2) Jerusalem was troubled. Even old Herod on the throne was disturbed. By the way, the record does not give us the number of wise men who came. I think there may have been three hundred of them at least, probably more than that. I doubt that three wise men would excite Jerusalem, but three hundred would. They had come because *they* had heard.

The Queen of Sheba, I think, excited even more interest that day when her caravan came inside the walls of Jerusalem. This woman, who comes out of the mysterious East, is not a wise man, but she is looking for wisdom. She is a queen who has wealth in abundance. You and I today have no notion of the wealth in the Orient of that day. We Americans bury our gold in a cave at Fort Knox, and nobody ever gets to see it. But it was on display in that day. This woman brought wealth with her, and when she arrived, the wealth and luxury of the Orient came inside the walls of Jerusalem. She had an entourage that attracted interest. She had servants and soldiers of every color of skin under the sun. I tell you, the people lined the streets, and no circus has ever attracted the interest that the Queen of Sheba did the day she arrived in Jerusalem.

Now she came with questions. It was the custom in that day for rulers to be asked riddles, what we call today conundrums—tricky, clever questions. Also she had questions that had to do with the heart, questions that related to her eternal destiny because this woman came out of spiritual darkness. Although her court was scintillating and sophisticated, though it was brilliant in many ways, it reflected spiritual darkness.

THE VISIT

The record tells us that she was absolutely overwhelmed and overcome by her encounter with King Solomon. First of all, Solomon answered all of her questions. He had answers for every one of them, and, "There was not anything hidden from the king, which he told her not" (1 Kings 10:3). In other words, she asked no question that he could not answer. It is said that many of the rulers of Egypt lost face because they were not able to answer questions that were put to them. Solomon never did. Solomon was able to answer all questions.

> *And when the queen of Sheba had seen the wisdom of Solomon, and the house that he had built, and the food of his table, and the sitting of his servants, and the attendance of his ministers, and their apparel; his cupbearers also, and their apparel; and his ascent by which he went up into the house of the Lord, there was no more spirit in her.* (2 Chronicles 9:3–4)

Look at this for just a moment. The first thing that impressed her was that he was able to answer all of her questions. The second thing was the tremendous organization and display that he had there. Everywhere she turned, not only pomp and ceremony, but also originality.

How we need originality today. There are too many folk trying to imitate instead of having an impartation of life and translating that in their own way. A very fine young preacher who was a former student of mine is having a lot of trouble, I understand. A friend came and talked to me about him because he is tremendously interested in him. He said to me, "Do you know what his trouble is? He's attempting to imitate." And he told me who he is imitating. So I went and talked to this young preacher. I said, "Look, the fellow you're imitating is all right, but you ought to be yourself for the simple reason that you're better as an original than you are as an imitation. In fact, all of us are." God has made each of us an original; let's just be ourselves. How we need originality today!

A fellow came into his office one morning bragging, "Do you know what my wife said to me this morning? She said I was a model husband!" After saying that to several people, finally someone asked him, "Have you ever looked up in the dictionary to see what *model* means?" "No," he said. "Well, you go look it up." So he went to the dictionary and found the meaning to be "a small imitation of the real article." He was a model husband! And, may I say, we have too many small imitations of the real article. We need today that which is original.

Hollywood is dying for the want of genius. They haven't had an original idea in twenty years, and that is the reason smut has become a synonym for sophistication. A great many people do not seem to know the difference, and they go for that dirty, filthy sort of thing, thinking they are being sophisticated. It is just a lack of genius and a lack of ability today.

When the Queen of Sheba came to Jerusalem, I can imagine that she said, "Wow, I have never seen anything like this before! Solomon, you certainly didn't copy anybody!" I'm sure Solomon said, "No, my father David knew God, and God blessed him and revealed these things to him. Now He has blessed me, His son, as I've attempted to carry out the things He wanted done."

Oh, friend, how God wants us today to come to the place where He can use us, and use us in an original way!

Now we are told the third thing which impressed the Queen of Sheba: "His ascent by which he went up into the house of the LORD." *Ascent* is a very unfortunate translation because in the record in 1 Kings 10:5 the Hebrew word is *olah,* meaning "burnt offerings." She was impressed by his burnt offerings which he offered to God. Here in Chronicles the word *ascent* is *aliyyah,* meaning "uppermost place." We are told that in the temple the king had a private way by which he went up to the altar, but after he got there he was on the same plane as everybody else. That impressed her because down in her country she was far above the level of the crowds. But Solomon, even after he went up his way, stood by that burnt altar just like any other sinner stands before God.

That burnt altar speaks eloquently of the cross of Christ. It is the finest picture of the cross of Christ we have in the Old Testament. That burnt altar was the place where sacrificial animals were burned. These burnt sacrifices which so impressed her speak of the person of Christ, of *who* He is; and the sin offering put there speaks of the work of Christ. This woman found when she came to Jerusalem that the living and true God was approached only through a sacrifice. A substitute was offered. Even a king had to come as a sinner and stand with the lowest subjects to receive salvation from God. That, I believe, is the way the Queen of Sheba came. The thing that God has revealed is that there is a righteousness which He provides.

I have been deeply impressed by this Scripture:

But now the righteousness of God apart from the law is manifested, being witnessed by the law and the prophets. (Romans 3:21)

You see, the Old Testament pictured this truth in the burnt offering in a way that the Queen of Sheba could understand. All of this was pointing to Christ and a righteousness God was providing for a king or for any sinner that He might accept him into His presence. That righteousness would be through the sacrifice of Another.

> *Even the [gift of] righteousness of [from] God which is by faith of Jesus Christ unto all and upon all them that believe; for there is no difference. For all have sinned, and come short of the glory of God.* (Romans 3:22–23)

We all stand on the same plane and all must come, and all *can* receive this righteousness. It is my opinion that the Queen of Sheba came to know the living and the true God when she came to Jerusalem. The Lord Jesus, when He was here, said this to the generation around Him:

> *The queen of the south shall rise up in the judgment with this generation, and shall condemn it: for she came from the farthest parts of the earth to hear the wisdom of Solomon; and, behold, a greater than Solomon is here.* (Matthew 12:42)

As Jesus spoke, the people were turning their backs upon Him, but *she* came from the ends of the earth to learn of Him.

A STEP OF FAITH

Now what brought her to Jerusalem? As I have said, she heard. But what was it that caused her to act? I suggest several things. First of all, it was her curiosity, I think, that prompted her visit. She kept hearing. Visitors would come to her court with news of Jerusalem. An envoy would report, "We have been to Jerusalem." She'd say, "I've been hearing about Jerusalem. Did you go to the temple?" They would say, "We sure did. It was a thrilling experience to go into that temple. We were there on one of their feast days. Wish you could have heard them singing their song. It was tremendous! And there was the altar, and, oh, there was gold, there was silver. It was beautiful. And the service, say, it was wonderful." The Queen of Sheba would say, "Yes, I've been hearing about that, and I would like to see it for myself. Maybe one of these days I can make the trip." Curiosity.

Now curiosity is something that not only women have—men have it also. If you don't believe it, make an experiment. When I worked on the *Commercial Appeal* in Memphis, there was a columnist who made a bet one day that he could go out on the street and stop traffic by doing nothing in the world but look up. So he got two fellows off the city desk to go with him to the corner of Main and Madison in Memphis. They stepped out there and the three of them looked up. Before long, a half dozen people had stopped. After they got about twenty there, they slipped out of the crowd and went across the street to watch. For the next thirty minutes traffic was jammed with everybody coming and looking up, and there wasn't a thing to see! Curiosity.

The Queen of Sheba was, I am sure, curious. But there was more than that.

The second thing that motivated the Queen of Sheba was a spirit of inquiry and interest, more than just curiosity. When they told her about an altar where sinners could come—queens could come, kings could come, everybody could come—to receive forgiveness of sins, she had an interest. She said, "I think I'd like to go. I think we'll arrange a trip."

Then there is a third reason. Down deep in her heart there was dissatisfaction and hunger. Here was a queen on a throne. She had everything her little heart wanted. And if there was anything she desired, she got it. Yet there was frustration. She never knew what real satisfaction was. She said to King Solomon:

> *It was a true report which I heard in mine own land of thine acts, and of thy wisdom; howbeit, I believed not their words, until I came, and mine eyes had seen it. And, behold, the one half of the greatness of thy wisdom was not told me; for thou exceedest the fame that I heard.* (2 Chronicles 9:5–6)

Although she believed in a way, she thought it couldn't be true, but she believed enough to come. And, my beloved, that is all any sinner needs, just faith enough to come to Christ. Paul said something so important to the Colossians:

> *For this cause we also, since the day we heard it, do not cease to pray for you, and to desire that ye might be filled with the knowledge of his will in all wisdom and spiritual understanding.* (Colossians 1:9)

But, what is His will? His Word—that you might be filled with the knowledge of His Word. The Queen of Sheba didn't believe very much, but she came. And when she got there she said, "The half wasn't told me!" Yet she believed enough to come.

My friend, you don't need much faith just to come to Jesus Christ and say, "I'll take You as my Savior, although I've got a lot of questions and a lot of problems." Paul prayed that the Colossians might be filled with the knowledge (the *epignosis,* meaning "super-knowledge"). Do you know what kind of knowledge that is? That is the kind of knowledge God gives you. After you have come to Christ, He makes these things real to you.

Faith is not a leap in the dark. It is not just a "hope so." It's not just a betting of your life on God. It is not shutting your eyes and taking a step. Faith rests upon real knowledge. When any man has faith enough just to reach out and take Christ as Savior, the Spirit of God makes these things *real* to him. I remember when I first came to Him, how little I knew, how little I believed. I've passed that stage now. There are a lot of things I don't even argue about anymore. He has made them real to my heart. That to me is the greatest knowledge you can have, to believe Him and then to have Him in turn make these things real to you.

Oh, if you have that dissatisfaction and hunger, just enough to come to Christ and take Him as your Savior, He will do the rest for you. Paul says in effect, "I'm praying that you might be filled with that super-knowledge of His Word, that these things might be made real to you."

A man wanted to argue with me the other day. He said, "How do you know the Bible is the Word of God?" I said, "Brother, God has made that thing real to me a thousand different ways. I heard what you've got to say years ago, and I must admit I had doubts then, but God has made His Word so real to me today that it is more real than any of these objections." And God will make it real to you, my friend. This is what Paul is talking about.

The Queen of Sheba came, and I see something else that caused her to come. Self-sacrifice. She came probably two thousand miles, and in that day they were not running the Super Chief, nor had the super jets been put in operation. When she came, it was a long and arduous trip which took months of planning. It was a hard, dangerous trip, but she undertook it in order to come to Jerusalem.

Today God does not ask you to make a trip anywhere.

But the righteousness which is of faith speaketh on this wise, Say not in thine heart, Who shall ascend into heaven? (that is, to bring Christ down from above); or, Who shall descend into the deep? (that is, to bring up Christ again from the dead). But what saith it? The word is near thee, even in thy mouth, and in thy heart; that is, the word of faith, which we preach: that if thou shalt confess with thy mouth the Lord Jesus, and shalt believe in thine heart that God hath raised him from the dead, thou shalt be saved. For with the heart man be-

lieveth unto righteousness; and with the mouth confession is made unto salvation. (Romans 10:6–10)

Today you do not have to make a long trip to Jerusalem. You do not even have to go across the street. He is available to you. You have no excuse. The Queen of Sheba is going to rise up someday and judge America according to Matthew 12:42. She came two thousand miles to get saved, but many Americans with the gospel coming right into their homes reject Christ. She will judge them someday. It is close to you today, my friend. You do not have to go anywhere. Sit right where you are and receive Him.

3

AN X-RAY OF THE CROSS

(Psalm 22)

*1 My God, my God, why hast thou forsaken me?
Why art thou so far from helping me, and from the
words of my roaring?*

*2 O my God, I cry in the daytime, but thou hearest
not; and in the night season, and am not silent.*

*3 But thou art holy, O thou that inhabitest the
praises of Israel.*

*4 Our fathers trusted in thee: they trusted, and thou
didst deliver them.*

*5 They cried unto thee, and were delivered: they
trusted in thee, and were not confounded.*

*6 But I am a worm, and no man; a reproach of men,
and despised of the people.*

There are several Scriptures with which I never feel adequate to deal. This is one of them. When we come to Psalm 22 I feel that we are standing on holy ground and we should take off our spiritual shoes. This psalm is called the Psalm of the Cross. It is so named because it describes more accurately and minutely the crucifixion of Christ than does any other portion of the Word of God. It corresponds, of course, to the twenty-second chapter of Genesis and the fifty-third chapter of Isaiah.

We have many messianic psalms which are pictures of Christ. The first psalm, for instance, is a portrait of Christ in His character—who He is, His life, His practice. But in Psalm 22 we have an x-ray which penetrates into His thoughts and into His inner life. In this psalm we see the anguish of His passion. His soul is laid bare. In the Gospels is recorded the historical fact of His death and some of the events which attended His crucifixion, but only in Psalm 22 are His thoughts revealed. It has been the belief of many scholars that the Lord Jesus, while on the cross, actually quoted the entire twenty-second psalm. I concur in this, because the seven last sayings that are given in the Gospels either appear in this psalm or the psychological background for them is here.

It is the custom in many churches to conduct a Good Friday service in which seven ministers bring messages from the seven last sayings of Christ from the cross. In the course of fifteen years, I have heard over one hundred men deal with these seven words. It is always a spiritual feast to hear how each man develops the subject, and always there are many new and profitable thoughts presented. However, we shall attempt to encompass all seven sayings in one message. And instead of standing beneath the cross and listening to Him, we are going to hang on the cross with Him. We shall view the crucifixion of Christ from a new position—from the cross itself. And we can look with Him on those beneath His cross, as He was hanging there, and see what went on in His heart and in His mind. We shall see what occurred in His soul as He became the sacrifice for the sins of the world. As He was suspended there between heaven and earth, He became the ladder let down from heaven to this earth so that men might have a way to God.

We were there, if you please, on that cross as He was made sin for us—He who knew no sin; that we might be made the righteousness of God through Him. We were as truly on that cross when He died as we today are *in* Christ by faith. Peter put it like this:

> *Who his own self bare our sins in his own body on the tree, that we, being dead to sins, should live unto righteousness: by whose stripes ye were healed.* (1 Peter 2:24)

Healed from sin!

MY GOD, MY GOD, WHY HAST THOU FORSAKEN ME? (Matthew 27:46)

Psalm 22 opens with the plaintive and desperate cry of this poor, lone man, forsaken of God. There has been an attempt made to play down the stark reality and the bitter truth that He was forsaken of God. I hold an article written by a local minister who takes the position that Jesus was not forsaken. He attempts to translate *"Eli, Eli lama sabachthani"* to mean "My God, my God, for this was I kept." His authority is the Peshitta, or the Syriac version. However, the Peshitta is not a good manuscript. It never has been used by any reputable translator, for it is not a reliable translation. Evidently it was made by some who had gone into a heresy at the very beginning. The value of it is that it throws light, in many places, on the customs in Palestine during that period. I have used it in that connection on several occasions, but never would I accept the translation. Actually, the Hebrew is very clear, and the Greek is very clear, and the Aramaic is very clear—in each language the cry means that Jesus was forsaken of God.

Now this is something I want to emphasize from the very beginning: we have here a record of His *human suffering*. We see Him hanging there as a man, "the Lamb of God that taketh away the sin of the world."

We get more light on this by turning to the Epistle to the Hebrews:

> *But we see Jesus, who was made a little lower than the angels* [a little lower than the angels? Yes, made a man. Why?] *for the suffering of death, crowned with glory and honour; that he by the grace of God should taste death for every man.* (Hebrews 2:9)

That is what we are looking at—the one who left heaven's glory and became a man. He became a man to reveal God, yes, that is true, but most of all to redeem man.

> *Forasmuch then as the children are partakers of flesh and blood, he also himself likewise took part of the same; that through death he might destroy him that had the power of death, that is, the devil.* (Hebrews 2:14)

He could save no one by His life. It was His sacrificial death that saves.

> *And deliver them who through fear of death were all their lifetime subject to bondage. For verily he took not on him the nature of angels; but he took on him the seed of Abraham. . . . For in that he himself hath suffered being tempted, he is able to succour* [help] *them that are tempted.* (Hebrews 2:15–16, 18)

We see the man Christ Jesus on the cross as the perfect man. He had learned to rest upon God. He had learned to trust Him in all that He did. He said, "I do always the things that please Him." But yonder in that desperate and despairing hour He is abandoned of God. There is no place to turn either on the human plane or on the divine. He has no place to go. The man Christ Jesus is forsaken. No other ever has had to experience that. No one. He alone.

Why did God forsake Him? Turn back to Psalm 22:

But thou art holy, O thou that inhabitest the praises of Israel. (Psalm 22:3)

Why was He forsaken of God? Because on the cross in those last three hours, in the impenetrable darkness, He was made sin.

> *But none of the ransomed ever knew*
> *How deep were the waters crossed;*
> *Nor how dark was the night that*
> *the Lord passed through*
> *Ere He found His sheep that was lost.*

He was forsaken for a brief moment. The paradox is that at that very moment God was in Christ reconciling the world unto Himself. And the Lord Jesus Himself said,

Behold, the hour cometh, yea, is now come, that ye shall be scattered, every man to his own, and shall leave me alone: and yet I am not alone, because the Father is with me. (John 16:32)

The Father was with Him when He was in prison. The Father was with Him when He was being beaten. The Father was with Him when they nailed Him to the cross. But in those last three hours He made His soul an offering for sin, and it pleased the Father to bruise Him.

Forsaken.

My friend, you do not know what that is, and I do not know what it is to be forsaken of God. The vilest man on this earth today is not forsaken of God. Anyone can turn to Him. But when Christ took my sin upon Himself, He was forsaken of God.

My God, my God, why hast thou forsaken me?

It is not the *why* of impatience. It is not the *why* of despair. It is not the *why* of doubt. It is the human cry of intense suffering, aggravated by the anguish of His innocent and holy life. That awful and agonizing cry of the loneliness of His passion! He was alone. He was alone with the sins of the world upon Him.

> *. . . Why art thou so far from helping me, and from the words of my roaring?* (Psalm 22:1)

Roaring? Yes. At His trial He was silent, *"As a sheep before her shearers is dumb, so he openeth not his mouth* (Isaiah 53:7)."* When they beat Him, He said nothing, when they nailed Him to the cross, He did not whimper. But when God forsook Him, He roared like a lion. It was a roar of pain. Have you ever been in the woods when dogs attacked an animal? Have you heard the shriek of that animal? There is nothing quite like it. And that is what the writer is attempting to convey to us here. I think that shriek from the cross rent the rocks, for it had been His voice that had created them. Now the Creator was suffering! On that cross He cried like a wounded animal, not sounding as a human cry but like a wild, roaring lion. It was the plaintive shriek and the wail of unutterable woe as our sins were pressed down upon Him.

Now notice verse 6 of Psalm 22:

> *But I am a worm. . . .*

What does He mean when He says, "I am a worm"? He has roared like a lion, but now He says, "I am a worm." It is because He has reached the very lowest place.

> *He is despised and rejected of men; a man of sorrows, and acquainted with grief: and we hid as it were our faces from him; he was despised, and we esteemed him not.* (Isaiah 53:3)

"I am a worm." The interesting thing is that the word used here for worm means the coccus worm, which was used by the Hebrews in dyeing all the curtains of the tabernacle scarlet red. When He said, "I am a worm," He meant more than that He had reached the lowest level. It was He who had said, "Though your sins be as scarlet, they shall be as white as snow." Only His blood, my friend, can rub out that dark, deep spot in your life.

Lady Macbeth, sleepwalking that night, went up and down rubbing her hands, having committed murder after murder. She said, "All the perfumes of Arabia will not sweeten this little hand." And she was right, they could not. She seemed to be continually washing her hands as she rubbed them together, and she cried, "Out damned spot! Out, I say!"

My friend, there is only one thing that will take the spot of sin out of your life, and that is the blood of Christ. The blood of the Lord Jesus, God's Son, cleanses from all sin. Only His blood.

FATHER, FORGIVE THEM (Luke 23:34)

Will you look at that victim on the cross? His suffering is intensified by that brutal mob of hardened spectators beneath Him. Look through His eyes and see what He sees.

> *All they that see me laugh me to scorn: they shoot out the lip, they shake the head, saying, He trusted on the LORD that he would deliver him: let him deliver him, seeing he delighted in him.* (Psalm 22:7–8)

Some criminals have been so detested that they have been taken from jail and lynched by a mob. But while the criminal was being executed, the mob would disperse. Tempers were cooled and emotions were assuaged. But not this crowd! I think the lowest thing that ever has been said of religion was said of these Pharisees when the Lord Jesus Christ was dying: "And sitting down they watched him there." You have to be low to do that. In fact, you cannot get lower than that! The venom and vileness of the human heart was being poured out like an open sewer as they remained there and ridiculed Him in His death. After a snake has put its deadly fangs into its victim and emitted its poison, it will slither away in the grass. But not this crowd, and not the human heart in rebellion against God.

Here is where Jesus said, "Father, forgive them; for they know not what they do." If He had not said that, this crowd would have committed the unpardonable sin. But they did not—He asked forgiveness for their sin. We know that the centurion in charge of the execution was saved, and a whole company of Pharisees, including Saul of Tarsus who probably was in this crowd, were saved.

WOMAN, BEHOLD THY SON! (John 19:26)

Now as He looks over the crowd He sees not only eyes of hate and antagonism, but He sees eyes of love. He sees His mother with John down there. "There stood by the cross of Jesus his mother," according to John's record. As Jesus looks at her, do you want to know what went on in His heart? He went back to Bethlehem at the time He was born. And He says to the Father,

But thou art he that took me out of the womb: thou didst make me hope when I was upon my mother's breasts. I was cast upon thee from the womb: thou art my God from my mother's belly. (Psalm 22:9–10)

Now to His mother He says, "Woman, behold thy son!" Yonder at the wedding at Cana in Galilee, she had asked Him to do something to show that He was the Messiah, that she was right when she said He was virgin born. She wanted Him to reveal Himself at this wedding. His answer to her at that time was, "Woman, what have I to do with thee? mine hour is not yet come." But there hanging on the cross, "Woman, behold thy son!" His hour has come. The reason for His coming into the world is now being accomplished. This is the most important hour in the history of the world!

Then His attention moves back to those who are doing the crucifying.

> *Many bulls have compassed me: strong bulls of Bashan have beset me round.* (Psalm 22:12)

Describing these soldiers that were crucifying Him, He says they are like the bulls of Bashan, but He does not stop with that, for He is being devoured by wild animals—that is what His tormentors had become:

> *They gaped upon me with their mouths, as a ravening and a roaring lion.* (Psalm 22:13)

He is talking about Rome now—Rome crucified Him. He compares them to a roaring lion, for the lion was the picture of Rome.

Now notice His condition:

> *I am poured out like water, and all my bones are out of joint: my heart is like wax; it is melted in the midst of my bowels.* (Psalm 22:14)

This accurate description of crucifixion is remarkable when you consider that crucifixion was unknown when this psalm was written. The Roman Empire was not even in existence, and it was Rome that instituted execution by crucifixion. Yet here is a picture of a man dying by crucifixion!

"I am poured out like water"—the excessive perspiration of a dying man out in that sun.

"All my bones are out of joint"—the horrible thing about crucifixion was that when a man began to lose blood, his strength ebbed from him, and all his bones slipped out of joint. That is an awful thing. It was terrible, terrible suffering.

Then He says something that is indeed strange, "My heart is like wax." He died of a broken heart. Many doctors have said that a ruptured heart would have produced what John meticulously recorded, "I saw that Roman soldier put the spear in His side, and there came out blood and water"—not just blood, but blood and water. John took note of that and recorded it. May I say to you, Jesus died of a broken heart.

I THIRST (John 19:28)

As He is hanging there ready to expire, with excessive perspiration pouring from Him, He suffers the agony of thirst.

My strength is dried up like a potsherd; and my tongue cleaveth to my jaws; and thou hast brought me into the dust of death. (Psalm 22:15)

Down beneath the cross they hear Him say, "I thirst."

For dogs have compassed me: the assembly of the wicked have enclosed me: they pierced my hands and my feet. (Psalm 22:16)

"Dog" was the name for Gentiles. The piercing of His hands and feet is an accurate description of crucifixion.

I may tell [count] all my bones: they look and stare upon me. They part my garments among them, and cast lots upon my vesture. (Psalm 22:17–18)

He was crucified naked. It is difficult for us, in this age of nudity and pornography, to comprehend the great humiliation He suffered by hanging nude on the cross. They had taken His garments and gambled for ownership. My friend, He went through it all, crucified naked, that you might be clothed with the righteousness of Christ and stand before God throughout the endless ages of eternity.

FATHER, INTO THY HANDS I COMMEND MY SPIRIT (Luke 23:46)

But be not thou far from me, O LORD: O my strength, haste thee to help me. Deliver my soul from the sword; my darling from the power of the dog. (Psalm 22:19–20)

The word *darling* is better translated *my only one*—"This is my beloved son." "Deliver my soul from the sword; my only one from the power of the dog." Jesus is saying, "Father, into thy hands I commend my spirit."

Save me from the lion's mouth: for thou hast heard me from the horns of the unicorns. (Psalm 22:21)

Again He is saying, "Father, into thy hands I commend my spirit."

One of the most remarkable statements is this, "Thou hast heard me from the horns of the unicorns." To express intensity in the Hebrew, the plural is used—horns of the unicorns; but the thought is *one horn*.

Now for many years it was thought that the unicorn was a mythical animal, but recent investigation has revealed that it was an animal a size smaller than the elephant, very much like the rhinoceros, sometimes called the wild bull. Vicious and brutal, every one of them was a killer. And the thing that identified them was the fact that they had *one horn.* "Thou hast heard me from the horns of the unicorns"—*uni* means one—one horn. To me, my beloved, that is remarkable indeed, because the cross on which the Lord Jesus Christ was crucified was not the shaped cross that we see today. We think of a cross made of an upright with a crosspiece. Nowhere does Scripture so describe it.

There are two Greek words that are translated by the English word *cross*. One of them is the word *stauros*. You find it used in several places. For instance:

> **Thou that destroyest the temple, and buildest it in three days, save thyself. If thou be the Son of God, come down from the cross.** (Matthew 27:40)

The word *cross* is *stauros*, meaning one piece. It is interesting how accurate Scripture is, but how tradition has woven into it our thinking. Paul used the word *stauros* when he wrote:

> **For the preaching of the cross [stauros]** *is to them that perish foolishness; but unto us which are saved it is the power of God.* (1 Corinthians 1:18)

The second Greek word is *xulon*, which is translated by the English word *cross* or *tree*. It simply means a piece of wood. Paul also used this word:

> **And when they had fulfilled all that was written of him, they took him down from the tree [xulon],** *and laid him in a sepulchre.* (Acts 13:29)

They took Him down from the tree! Does he mean an upright with a crosspiece?

Now I am perfectly willing to go along with the popularly accepted shape of a cross, but for the sake of accuracy and to appreciate the exactness of this psalm, we need to brush aside tradition for a moment. Jesus said, "Thou hast heard me from the horns of the unicorns [the cross]. Into thy hands I commend my spirit."

Another thing that amazes me is that this word *xulon*, translated "tree" or "cross," is mentioned in the twenty-second chapter of Revelation as the tree of life! I believe that the tree on which Jesus died will be there, alive, throughout the endless ages of eternity, to let you and me know what it cost to redeem us.

Now when we come to the twenty-second verse of this psalm, we see a radical change, a bifurcation. We have had the sufferings of Christ described for us, now we see the glory that should follow.

> *I will declare thy name unto my brethren: in the midst of the congregation will I praise thee.* (Psalm 22:22)

I think that He said this entire psalm on the cross. He did not die defeated, for when He reached the very end He said that this is the gospel that will be witnessed to. "I will declare thy name unto my brethren." And I see Peter in the midst of the Sanhedrin, composed of both Pharisees and Sadducees, saying to them, "There is none other name under heaven given among men, whereby we must be saved" (Acts 4:12). I will declare thy name unto my brethren.

TO DAY SHALT THOU BE WITH ME IN PARADISE (Luke 23:43)

> *My praise shall be of thee in the great congregation: I will pay my vows before them that fear him. The meek shall eat and be satisfied: they shall praise the LORD that seek him: your heart shall live forever.* (Psalm 22:25–26)

The thief on the cross said, "Lord, remember me when thou comest into thy kingdom." Christ says, "I'll pay my vows: today shalt thou be with me in paradise." The redeemed shall be there to praise, and that includes the thief He was taking with Him that very day. Although he was a man unfit to even live down here, according to Rome's standard, the Lord Jesus makes him fit for heaven by His death on the cross.

IT IS FINISHED (John 19:30)

There is a seventh word; it is His last.

They shall come, and shall declare his righteousness unto a people that shall be born, that he hath done this. (Psalm 22:31)

"To a people that shall be born" includes you, my friend.

They shall declare *His* righteousness—not your righteousness, for God says it is as filthy rags in His sight. How will they declare His righteousness? "That he hath done this." Some would translate it, "It is finished," the last word He spoke on the cross. And when He said it, it was but one word—*Tetelestai!* Finished! Your redemption is a completed package, and He presents it to you wrapped up with everything in it. He doesn't want you to bring your do-it-yourself kit along. He does not need that. When He died on the cross He provided a righteousness that would satisfy a holy God. All He asks of you is to receive this package, this gift of God, which is eternal life in Christ Jesus.

If you reject it, God must treat you as He treated His Son when He cried, "My God, my God, why hast thou forsaken me?" I am not here to argue about the temperature of hell; it will be hell for any man to be forsaken of God. Jesus Christ went through it that you might *never* have to utter that cry.

Psalm 22 reveals the heart of our Savior as He was made a sin offering in our behalf. He completed the transaction in triumph. He offers to us a finished redemption. We never shall be worthy of it, we cannot earn it, we cannot buy it—we must receive it as a gift. Almost two thousand years ago the Lord Jesus Christ did all that was needed to save us.

It is *done!*
Tetelestai!
Finished!

4

WORLD DOMINION: WHOSE WILL IT BE?

The Times of the Gentiles

(Daniel 2)

There are two worldwide kingdoms ahead of us, and we may be closer to them than we think we are. The first will be the kingdom of Antichrist, set up by man's philosophy and man's psychology. It will deify human beings and attempt to prove that they can unite and bring about a world of order, peace, and equality without God.

Because God instituted moral absolutes to govern man, man claims that Utopia can come only through the rejection of these absolutes. It is this kingdom that the Lord Jesus will destroy at His coming. All of man's supposed superiority will lie in the ashes and dust of the fallen empires which will be leveled by the Stone that smashes the image and grinds it to powder.

Gentiles have not done a very good job of running the world. We can see the beginning of this in the book of Daniel, dating way back to around 600 B.C. You and I have moved down pretty close to the end of Gentile rule, to a day when the Lord Jesus Christ will come forward and take the scepter of world dominion back into His own hands. The story of the "times of the Gentiles" is remarkably told in the chapter before us.

And in the second year of the reign of Nebuchadnezzar, Nebuchadnezzar dreamed dreams, wherewith his spirit was troubled, and his sleep brake from him.

Then the king commanded to call the magicians, and the astrologers, and the sorcerers, and the Chaldeans, for to show the king his dreams. So they came and stood before the king.

And the king said unto them, I have dreamed a dream, and my spirit was troubled to know the dream.

Then spake the Chaldeans to the king in Syriack [Aramaic], O king, live for ever: tell thy servants the dream, and we will show the interpretation.

The king answered and said to the Chaldeans, The thing is gone from me. . . . (Daniel 2:1–5)

Because of this translation, the impression has been given that the king had forgotten his dream and could not recall it. That, of course, is not true. He did know what his dream was. What he said is better translated "The word is gone forth from me," or putting it another way, "The word from me is sure." The king recognized that his wise men were hedging, they were stalling for time. He said in effect, "I want you to know that the thing that I've said is *sure,* my decision is firm. I do not intend to tell you the dream; I intend for you to tell *me* the dream and its meaning." Of course he knew what his dream was.

. . . If ye will not make known unto me the dream, with the interpretation thereof, ye shall be cut in pieces, and your houses shall be made a dunghill.

But if ye show the dream, and the interpretation thereof, ye shall receive of me gifts and rewards and great honour: therefore show me the dream, and the interpretation thereof.

They answered again and said, Let the king tell his servants the dream, and we will show the interpretation of it.

The king answered and said, I know of certainty that ye would gain the time, because ye see the thing is gone from me.

But if ye will not make known unto me the dream, there is but one decree for you: for ye have prepared lying and corrupt words to speak before me, till the time be changed: therefore tell me the dream, and I shall know that ye can show me the interpretation thereof. (Daniel 2:5–9)

You will recall the story of how Daniel now intervenes and God gives to him the dream and the interpretation of it. I think that Daniel asked God to let him dream the dream so he would know exactly what it was and that God actually caused him to dream the dream. Then he gets an audience with King Nebuchadnezzar, and here is his interpretation:

Thou, O king, sawest, and behold a great image. This great image, whose brightness was excellent, stood before thee; and the form thereof was terrible.

This image's head was of fine gold, his breast and his arms of silver, his belly and his thighs of brass,

His legs of iron, his feet part of iron and part of clay.

Thou sawest till that a stone was cut out without hands, which smote the image upon his feet that were of iron and clay, and brake them to pieces.

Then was the iron, the clay, the brass, the silver, and the gold, broken to pieces together, and became like the chaff of the summer threshingfloors; and the wind carried them away, that no place was found for them: and the stone that smote the image became a great mountain, and filled the whole earth.

This is the dream; and we will tell the interpretation thereof before the king.

Thou, O king, art a king of kings: for the God of heaven hath given thee a kingdom, power, and strength, and glory.

And wheresoever the children of men dwell, the beasts of the field and the fowls of the heaven hath he given into thine hand, and hath made thee ruler over them all. Thou art this head of gold.

And after thee shall arise another kingdom inferior to thee, and another third kingdom of brass, which shall bear rule over all the earth.

And the fourth kingdom shall be strong as iron: forasmuch as iron breaketh in pieces and subdueth all things: and as iron that breaketh all these, shall it break in pieces and bruise.

And whereas thou sawest the feet and toes, part of potters' clay, and part of iron, the kingdom shall be divided; but there shall be in it of the strength of the iron, forasmuch as thou sawest the iron mixed with miry clay.

And as the toes of the feet were part of iron, and part of clay, so the kingdom shall be partly strong, and partly broken.

And whereas thou sawest iron mixed with miry clay, they shall mingle themselves with the seed of men: but they shall not cleave one to another, even as iron is not mixed with clay.

And in the days of these kings shall the God of heaven set up a kingdom, which shall never be destroyed: and the kingdom shall not be left to other people, but it shall break in pieces and consume all these kingdoms, and it shall stand for ever.

Forasmuch as thou sawest that the stone was cut out of the mountain without hands, and that it brake in pieces the iron, the brass, the clay, the silver, and the gold; the great God hath made known to the king what shall come to pass hereafter: and the dream is certain, and the interpretation thereof sure. (Daniel 2:31–45)

May I say at the outset that the subject before us about "the times of the Gentiles" is not an invention of a propagandist or a monger of sensationalism. The subject may sound sensational, but it is actually that which our Lord Himself gave. In the Gospel of Luke our Lord used that expression in language like this:

> *And they shall fall by the edge of the sword, and shall be led away captive into all nations: and Jerusalem shall be trodden down of the Gentiles, until the times of the Gentiles be fulfilled.* (Luke 21:24)

The "times of the Gentiles" happens to be a period of time that you can pinpoint. You can identify the beginning of it, and you can project the ending of it—which is still yonder in the future. There are other expressions used in Scripture that are not synonymous to this at all, and we need to be very careful.

For instance, Paul spoke to the Roman Christians about the *fullness* of the Gentiles.

> *For I would not, brethren, that ye should be ignorant of this mystery, lest ye should be wise in your own conceits; that blindness in part is happened to Israel, until the fulness of the Gentiles be come in.* (Romans 11:25)

Now the *fullness* of the Gentiles is that period when God is calling out from among the Gentiles a people to His name. In Acts 15 we read that James got up before the early church which was one hundred percent Jewish, and in substance he said to them, "Men and brethren, the prophets speak of the fact that God is going to take out of the Gentiles a people to His name. And after that, He will return and will build again the tabernacle of David which is fallen down. Then all the Gentiles will call upon Him."

Now that time which is labeled here "the fulness of the Gentiles" is the period in which you and I are now living. It will end with the Rapture of the church.

Now you can see that the *fullness* of the Gentiles differs

from the *times* of the Gentiles, although they run concurrently part of the way. The *fullness* of the Gentiles ends at the Rapture; the *times* of the Gentiles continues on until Christ returns to the earth to establish His kingdom.

You will notice that our Lord linked the *times* of the Gentiles with the city of Jerusalem. He said,

> *. . . And Jerusalem shall be trodden down of the Gentiles, until the times of the Gentiles be fulfilled.* (Luke 21:24)

In other words, the period that is labeled the times of the Gentiles is the period in which Jerusalem is trampled underfoot by the Gentiles.

The beginning of the times of the Gentiles is something you can pinpoint in history. Actually, I do not think this is even a debatable point anymore in the study of prophecy. It began with Nebuchadnezzar. He is the first one to lay siege to Jerusalem and to destroy it after David had become king.

Nebuchadnezzar's invasion was several hundred years after David's reign, but you'll notice that Egypt is not included in the dream of Nebuchadnezzar as one of the world empires, and yet Egypt had been a great world empire.

Neither was the Assyrian empire included, though Assyria did lay siege to Jerusalem around 700 B.C. Isaiah 37 records God's deliverance of Judah, not permitting even one arrow of the Assyrian army to be shot into the city. God would not allow Assyria to take Jerusalem—He was holding them out to give His people a full opportunity to return to Him.

You see, when David had been king over Israel, God had said to him, "I'm going to give you an *everlasting* kingdom." He also said to David, "It will be a *worldwide* kingdom, not just over Palestine but over this entire earth." And you will find that the psalmists picked up this promise and that the prophets repeatedly spoke of it. For instance, let me direct your attention to only one Scripture, Isaiah 2:1–3, so you may see that this kingdom which the prophets talked about was not just confined to Palestine but that it was to be worldwide.

> *The word that Isaiah the son of Amoz saw concerning Judah and Jerusalem. And it shall come to pass in the last days, that the mountain of the LORD's house shall be established in the top of the mountains, and shall be exalted above the hills. . . .*

The kingdom shall be established in the top of the "mountains," meaning earthly kingdoms, and shall be exalted above the "hills," referring to the little nations.

> *. . . and all nations shall flow unto it. And many people shall go and say, Come ye, and let us go up to the mountain of the LORD, to the house of the God of Jacob; and he will teach us of his ways. . . .*

Now that prophecy can be multiplied, not only once, twice, or three times, but I believe that I could give you five hundred prophecies from the Old Testament concerning that kingdom which is yet to be established upon this earth —universal and everlasting. That kingdom was represented by the scepter of David, and God kept telling those who followed in David's line that if they continued in sin He would take that scepter away from them, away from them temporarily until the times of the Gentiles would be fulfilled. However, they did not listen to the prophets whom God sent to them, and our Lord Jesus reminded the Jews of His day of that fact. And so the day came when God took the scepter out of the hands of Jehoiakim, king of Judah, and He placed it into the hands of Nebuchadnezzar, king of Babylon. He took the scepter of worldwide rulership and put it into Gentile hands. My friend, that was well over twenty-five hundred years ago, and that scepter today is still in the hands of the Gentiles.

The scepter represents world rulership, if you please. And this man Nebuchadnezzar found himself, overnight, a world ruler. He had defeated Necho, king of Egypt, and then was warring yonder in the delta of the Nile and was overcoming it—everything fell before him—when news came to him of the death of his father, Nabopolassar, which made this man Nebuchadnezzar the undisputed ruler of the world. Since he had overcome everything, a little tribal deity up in Judah by the name of Jehovah didn't amount to very much, he thought, so he could overcome there also. Who was to stand in his way?

When Nebuchadnezzar returned to Babylon, he could look over that great city that boasted a civilization second to none. To this day we have not presented to the world a civilization any greater than the Babylonian. And there came a question into his mind and to his heart about the future: *Here all of a sudden I find myself a world ruler. In my hand has been placed a scepter. It has come from somewhere. Who will it go to and what will happen to it? What will be the final outcome?* Do you know that after about twenty-five hundred or three thousand years of human history since Nebuchadnezzar, the world is still wondering about that? Well, we have the answer in this image.

So God spoke to this king through a dream one night. He answered his questions to let him know the future and also to let him know that these despised people whom he had brought into captivity were still His *chosen* people. It would be one of them who would be the instrument to reveal to the king the vision and the interpretation of it.

Now the man had a dream. It was a dream that he could certainly recall. Don't ever think for one moment that Nebuchadnezzar would have forgotten *this* dream! He saw an image, tremendous and awesome. God spoke to him in the kind of language he understood—Babylon was the very fountainhead of all idolatry. I suppose that Babylon had as many idolatrous images as Memphis in Egypt had. In fact, all idolatry can be traced back to the Tower of Babel and this city of Babylon. You can see that God communicated to him by way of an image, a language he understood.

Nebuchadnezzar wondered about this great image that did nothing but just stand before him. There was no movement at all. It just stood there in its brightness—multicolored, polychrome, a multi-metallic image. He'd seen nothing like it. It was stupendous and awe inspiring. It was *fierce* in its countenance. It was that which would incite terror!

The king wondered about it and was so troubled he summoned his cabinet—but he wanted to make sure he would get accurate information. I think he said to himself, *I've been suspecting these wise men of getting free board here; they're just hangers on; they've just been giving me a lot of malarkey. I'm going to find out whether they're genuine or not.* When they came and stood before him, he said, "I had a dream, and I want you to know it's an important dream— you can be sure of that! I want you to tell me what the dream is, and then I want you to give me the interpretation of it." These wise men were the brain trust of Babylon. Because they couldn't come up with the answer, do not think that these men did not represent the best brains of the day, for they did. They said, "We can tell you the interpretation if you'll tell us the dream, but we don't know what the dream is."

And Nebuchadnezzar said, "You'll have to tell me the dream. Because I'm tremendously concerned about it, I'll not know that your interpetation is valid unless you can tell me the dream."

> *For this cause the king was angry and very furious, and commanded to destroy all the wise men of Babylon.*
> (Daniel 2:12)

This was Satan's effort, of course, to destroy Daniel because he had already become a conspicuous man, a man of purpose in that court. Daniel had been faithful to God, and the devil wanted to destroy him.

When word is brought to Daniel that all of the wise men are to be destroyed unless the dream can be given, this man Daniel with real confidence and faith in God asks for an audience with the king. When he is ushered into Nebuchadnezzar's presence, he says, "Just give me time and we'll give you the interpretation." The king says, "All right, if you think you can do it, young man, I'll give you the opportunity. I admire your spunk. If you feel that you can bring forth the dream, I'll be willing to wait." So Daniel goes and calls his three friends together, and they have a prayer meeting. I'll bet you this is the greatest prayer meeting ever to be held in the city of Babylon. They pray fervently that night. They lay hold of God that night, and God gives to Daniel in a night vision the dream and the interpretation of it. Then Daniel asks for another audience with Nebuchadnezzar, and the captain of the guard quickly ushers him in to the king. Daniel says in substance to the king, "I'm going to give you the dream and I'm going to give you the interpretation. But I want you to understand one thing: It's not because of anything in me. Don't give me credit for it. I want you to know that there is a God in heaven who reveals secrets."

By the way, I personally think that Nebuchadnezzar came to know that there is a God in heaven and became a converted man through this experience. I expect some day to meet him on Hallelujah Boulevard in heaven.

Now Daniel describes the dream, "You saw in your dream a great image." The minute he says that, I think Nebuchadnezzar's eyes light up. He might have been skeptical at first as he looked down on this young man: *He's rather presumptuous to think he can do a thing like this!* But the minute Daniel said to him, "You saw in your dream a great *image*," I think Nebuchadnezzar moved to the edge of his throne and said, "Go on, young man. You're on the right track."

Then Daniel continues, "You saw a great image of splendor. It was frightful to look upon. That image just stood there. It had a head of gold. It had chest and arms of silver. It had an abdomen and thighs of brass. It had legs of iron and feet of iron and miry clay."

Nebuchadnezzar says, "You're right. That's what I saw. That was my dream."

"And then you saw a *stone* cut out without hands. You saw it smite the image on the feet, and it pulverized it."

"That's right. That's what happened."

"Now I'll give you the interpretation of it." Daniel said first to him, "Thou, O king . . . thou art this head of gold." Then in substance he said, "What you have just seen, Nebuchadnezzar, is what God is going to do in the latter days, and God has given you the entire briefing of future rule. He set before you the course of Gentile domination down to the very end of Gentile world history."

Our Lord said, ". . . Jerusalem shall be trodden down of the Gentiles, until the times of the Gentiles be fulfilled" (Luke 21:24). For twenty-five hundred years the armies of these nations mentioned here, and others, have marched through Jerusalem. To me, one of the most thrilling things is this: When the United Nations made the Jewish population of Israel a nation, the Jews wanted above everything else the ancient city of Jerusalem. I held my breath when the United Nations was making that decision, and up to that time Russia and the United States hadn't agreed on anything in the United Nations, but they agreed they'd keep Jerusalem an *international* city. Jerusalem shall be trodden down of the Gentiles until the times of the Gentiles be fulfilled. Over there today Jerusalem is not in the hands of the little nation of Israel. They have only the new city; the old city is in the hands of the Arabs. Interesting, isn't it, my beloved, when you have the Word of God before you which has made this so crystal clear.

Now the kingdoms represented by the metals of the image are clearly identified. We do not have to speculate. Before we finish reading the book of Daniel we find that God actually names the first three kingdoms: Babylon; Media-Persia; Greece; and He so well describes the fourth kingdom as to leave no doubt that it is the Roman Empire.

Now I'm not going into details concerning these empires other than to say that historically each empire has followed the other exactly as God said it would, each one becoming a little stronger and a little larger than the other, but also each becoming a little inferior to the one that preceded it.

This man Nebuchadnezzar was an *absolute* monarch in the Babylonian Empire. He never asked anybody, not even his wife, about anything. He never shared rulership with anyone. When this man said, "Peace," there was peace in the world because he said it. A little bird didn't even chirp without his permission. (But do you want that kind of peace?)

After him came that oriental empire that dazzled the world, the Media-Persian Empire with all of its riches and oriental splendor. When Xerxes, lusting for power, moved toward the West, God stopped him at Thermopylae. The Greeks said the "gods" helped them there. But it wasn't gods (plural), it was singular—God did help the Greeks, in that He stopped the invading Media-Persian Empire. Three hundred ships were destroyed, and Xerxes lost a million men in that expedition.

Then God took the scepter of world dominion out of the hand of oriental rulers and passed it to Greece, placing it in the hands of the young man, Alexander the Great, who in just a brief span of eleven years conquered the world. But Greece couldn't hold it. There was a division after the death of Alexander at the age of thirty-two, and the empire was divided among his four generals. Then the scepter was passed to Rome, and Rome ruled.

The Media-Persian Empire had ruled from the Hellespont to the coral strands of India, from the top of the Euphrates down to the Persian Gulf, but now Rome comes on the scene and conquers the then-known world. All the way from the rockbound coast of Scotland to the burning sands of the Sahara Desert, all the way from the Rock of Gibraltar to the Euphrates River, the great Roman Empire ruled. It is the fourth and the last.

Now, my friend, although the boundaries widened, as you move down in history you see there is deterioration from one empire to the next empire. How different it is from man's outline of history! H. G. Wells wrote a book years ago entitled *The Outline of History*. He traced the history of man all the way up from the very beginning, from the Paleozoic to the Paleolithic to the Neolithic ages and up. It is onward and upward forever, bigger and better. That's the story of man according to H. G. Wells. But the interesting thing is, this man lived to see World War II, and before he died he said this: "The world has come to the end of its tether, and civilization has come to an end. We're standing on the brink, and we'll fall over one of these days." It doesn't sound like we're getting bigger and better. God said there would be no improvement.

God said there would be deterioration, and there is deterioration in four different aspects, as graphically depicted by the image. First of all, there's deterioration in the *worth* of the metals. Gold is certainly more valuable than iron, and it's gold to silver to brass to iron and then to clay.

Then there's deterioration in *position*. Nebuchadnezzar was the head of gold, and certainly the head occupies a more honored position than the foot occupies. There is deterioration here according to the clear-cut statement of Scripture: "After thee shall arise another kingdom *inferior* to thee." God makes it clear that each one in succession was to be inferior to the other.

Then there's something that Tregelles, the great Hebrew scholar, called attention to, and if you have studied chemistry—even one year of chemistry—you will recognize this: Even the *specific gravity* of these metals becomes less as you move down. All the way from the head of gold down to the feet of iron and clay there is deterioration.

Now there's something else that we must call to your attention here in conclusion which is very important. We are told that when Daniel appeared before king Nebuchadnezzar he said,

> *But there is a God in heaven that revealeth secrets, and maketh known to the king Nebuchadnezzar what shall be in the latter days. . . ."* (Daniel 2:28)

Note the expression "in the latter days," which has a very specific meaning. Those of you who are students of Scripture, and especially of prophecy, will recognize that it is an expression that occurs again and again in the Old Testament. You ought never to confuse the last days of Israel with the last days of the church. They're not the same at all. And the mentioning of the last days of Israel began way back, long before the people became a nation. When old Jacob was on his deathbed he called his twelve boys to come around him, and he made a prophecy concerning them, and here's what we're told in Genesis 49:1: "And Jacob called unto his sons, and said, Gather yourselves together, that I may tell you that which shall befall you in the last days"—the last days, in the latter times. You will find that the prophets all looked down the centuries to the *last* days. These last days concern the nation Israel.

Now what are these last days, these latter times, that God is talking about? Well, the fourth kingdom takes place, of course, in the latter days. That fourth kingdom is Rome. Now, my friend, I want you to look at something that is without doubt one of the most amazing things in the prophetic Word. No man could have guessed like this. There are only *four* worldwide kingdoms represented by these four different metals. There is first of all the head of gold, specifically stated to be Nebuchadnezzar in Daniel 2:38. There are the chest and the arms of silver, clearly identified as Media-Persia, and the brass abdomen and thighs of Greece, the Graeco-Macedonian Empire. Then there are the legs of iron with feet of iron and clay, the Roman Empire, and there are no more kingdoms after that. Rome is the last worldwide kingdom.

Now will you notice, Rome came to a dissolution about the fourth century A.D. It was in the fifth century that the barbarian hordes poured into the Roman Empire, and my ancestors and maybe yours were in those barbarian hordes. It's awful to think that you and I had barbarian ancestors, but we did. The barbarians poured into that empire. It fell apart because it was rotten to the core. It was a dictatorship, the like of which the world had never seen. Edward Gibbon, in his *Rise and Fall of the Roman Empire,* has written:

> The empire of the Romans filled the world, and when the empire fell into the hands of a single person, the world became a safe and dreary prison for his enemies. To resist was fatal and it was impossible to fly.

Robert Culver who more recently has written a brilliant book on Daniel says,

> Two millennia ago, Rome gave the world the ecumenical unity which the League of Nations and the United Nations organizations have sought to revive in our time. The modern attempts are not original at all (as many of our contemporaries suppose), but are revivals of the ancient Roman ideal which never since the time of Augustus Caesar has been wholly lost.

Rome did not end. Rome fell apart, that's all, just came loose at the seams. It never died. Rome lived on and Rome lives today in the broken fragments of many countries of Western Europe. Isn't it interesting that when Rome fell apart the barbarian hordes poured in? Attila the Hun sacked Rome, then looked about and was so awestruck by what he saw and realized he could not handle, that he took his army and left the city. There arose no *fifth* empire, and there hasn't for fifteen hundred years been a world empire. That's something to think about.

In the seventh century, out of the East came the Arab hordes—they came from both East and West under the crescent—Moslems, if you please, fanatics to the core and with a sword to convert the world. They almost destroyed the civilization of Western Europe at that time, what little there was. But *they built no empire.* The crescent of the Moslems was lifted over Constantinople, the capital of the eastern branch of the Roman Empire, and you would have expected one of the caliphs to ascend the throne of the Caesars, but none ascended it.

Tartars and Turks moved through Asia. Genghis Khan, Suleiman the Great—neither of them became a world ruler. Napoleon tried it, and on his way to Warsaw God stopped him with the weakest thing in the world, a snowflake. Bismarck, the iron chancellor of Germany, tried to put Western Europe together and revive the Roman Empire. He failed. William Hohenzollern tried, Hitler tried, and Mussolini tried. All failed.

I say to you, my beloved, there have been only *four* empires, and for fifteen hundred years the nations of Europe have been at each other's throats. There has been warring back and forth among those nations that composed the Roman Empire, and as of this writing the revived Roman Empire is somewhere down in the feet of the image where there are ten toes.

Now don't attempt to identify the nations represented by the toes. I can't; no one can yet. But they will fall into place after the church is removed at the Rapture. I have a friend who is always trying to locate which is which, and I like to kid him about it and say, "You remind me of going into the nursery and playing with a little baby's toes—this little piggy went to market, this little piggy stayed home. . . ." Although we cannot identify the nations that will compose the revived Roman Empire, at this point we are somewhere down in the time of the feet of the image. Notice again that there will be division. At the beginning there are two legs of iron and now there are ten toes representing division of empire. And they are made of clay and iron, the clay denoting weakness and iron denoting strength. You and I know that in Europe there are both today.

Do you know what Western Europe is waiting for at this hour? It waits for a man big enough and strong enough to come along and put Western Europe back together again, and they are making progress. Europe feels itself caught between two colossi, two great juggernauts—Russia on one side, the United States on the other—and the little nations of Europe are now wanting to get together. They've already come together; they have the Common Market. No longer do you have difficulty crossing over from Germany to France and from one country to another. Someone who had been in Europe this summer was telling me that it was just like going from one state to the other, lots easier than coming into California—nobody looks in your suitcase! They're breaking down the barriers. A brilliant young German said not long ago, "We are *European.*" Will that be the name of the new nation that will come out of this? Western Europe *will* come back together, and we're told in the Word of God that this last empire will be headed up by the Antichrist, for he alone will bring it back together again. And he will accomplish it in the *last days.*

This will end the times of the Gentiles, for when it comes back together it will defy God again. Remember, this is the empire that crucified our Lord Jesus on the cross. This empire in the days of Caesar Augustus sent out a decree that the whole *world* should be taxed. Boy! That sounds familiar, doesn't it? Mary had to go down from Nazareth to Bethlehem, because she was of the house and lineage of David, in order to enroll for the taxation made by Rome. And Rome will defy our Lord; Rome again will seek to destroy Him. Then He will come forth, and this time—it is His second coming that's before us—He is represented by the stone, the smiting stone.

Daniel continues,

> *Thou sawest till that a stone was cut out without hands,*
> *which smote the image upon his feet that were of iron*
> *and clay, and brake them to pieces. Then was the iron,*
> *the clay, the brass, the silver, and the gold, broken to*
> *pieces together, and became like the chaff of the sum-*
> *mer threshingfloors; and the wind carried them away,*
> *that no place was found for them: and the stone that*
> *smote the image became a great mountain, and filled*
> *the whole earth.* (Daniel 2:34–35)

Nebuchadnezzar beheld the image in awe and wonder. The stone, coming from beyond the environs of the image and without human origin or motivation, smote the image on the feet of iron and clay with such force that all the metals were pulverized. And a wind blew the dust of the image away, so that it entirely disappeared. Then the stone began to grow as a living stone, and it filled the whole world, taking the place of this image.

My friend, you and I are living in a world where men in the religious community have been saying for years that the church is going to convert the world, that the kingdom of God will be established by human effort. The Bible has been saying the contrary. When God is ready to set up His Kingdom, He won't need help from any church! This age in which we live will not end with a converted world. This age is to end by the catastrophic and cataclysmic coming of Jesus Christ to this earth to put down Gentile misrule and to take for Himself the scepter of world dominion. He is the smiting Stone of destruction.

The reason that Stone has not struck is that the last part of the prophecy has not quite yet been fulfilled. Antichrist is yet to appear, but God is holding him back. Europe is crying out for him. If any man will appear in Europe who can put the countries of the Roman Empire back together again, they'll not ask and they won't care whether he comes from heaven or hell. They'll take him if he will just promise to bring them together and give them a measure of peace, for that is exactly what the Antichrist will promise and accomplish for a brief time when he comes. But there's no real peace for this earth until Jesus comes.

In the meantime in patience our Lord is dealing with this world, and in mercy He's holding back the judgment. On an occasion when the Lord Jesus confronted the Pharisees, He said,

> *Therefore say I unto you, The kingdom of God shall be taken from you, and given to a nation bringing forth the fruits thereof. And whosoever shall fall on this stone shall be broken: but on whomsoever it shall fall, it will grind him to powder.* (Matthew 21:43–44)

My friend, if you fall upon this Stone, you can obtain mercy and you can be saved.

> *The Father loveth the Son, and hath given all things into his hand. He that believeth on the Son hath everlasting life: and he that believeth not the Son shall not see life; but the wrath of God abideth on him.* (John 3:35–36)

You and I have moved down pretty close to the end of the age, to a day coming when the Lord Jesus will come forward and take that scepter back into His own hands. And, friend, there will never be peace on this earth until that scepter is held by nail-pierced hands, until Jesus Christ rules on this earth. It's not until then that peace and righteousness will cover this earth as the waters cover the sea. That is the hope of the earth.

— 5 —

WHEN GOD BECAME MAN

(John 1:1–18)

———

1 In the beginning was the Word, and the Word was with God, and the Word was God.

2 The same was in the beginning with God.

3 All things were made by him; and without him was not any thing made that was made.

4 In him was life; and the life was the light of men.

5 And the light shineth in darkness; and the darkness comprehended it not.

6 There was a man sent from God, whose name was John.

7 The same came for a witness, to bear witness of the Light, that all men through him might believe.

8 He was not that Light, but was sent to bear witness of that Light.

9 That was the true Light, which lighteth every man that cometh into the world.

10 He was in the world, and the world was made by him, and the world knew him not.

11 He came unto his own, and his own received him not.

12 But as many as received him, to them gave he power to become the sons of God, even to them that believe on his name:

13 Which were born, not of blood, nor of the will of the flesh, nor of the will of man, but of God.

63

14 And the Word was made flesh, and dwelt among us, (and we beheld his glory, the glory as of the only begotten of the Father,) full of grace and truth.

15 John bare witness of him, and cried, saying, This was he of whom I spake, He that cometh after me is preferred before me: for he was before me.

16 And of his fulness have all we received, and grace for grace.

17 For the law was given by Moses, but grace and truth came by Jesus Christ.

18 No man hath seen God at any time; the only begotten Son, which is in the bosom of the Father, he hath declared him.

—Gospel of St. John 1:1–18

Our little earth revolves in a vast, dark universe. And on its surface storms are blowing—storms of hate, of violence, of rebellion and unbelief. Today we hear voices of so-called theologians saying, "There is nobody out there in the dark; God is dead." It reminds me of an old story concerning Mark Twain. A report went around that he had died. When someone asked him about it, he said, "Well, it is greatly exaggerated." My friend, to say that God is dead is greatly exaggerated and actually is only wishful thinking. Those who are saying it are like little boys whistling in the dark, trying to say how brave they are. There *is* Someone out there, and He is undisturbed by the little storms blowing across this planet, unchanged by our atomic age and space age and the shifting philosophy of men's minds. Over nineteen hundred years ago He came out of space, out of eternity to be identified with humanity. What relevance does His coming have to your life and to mine in this twentieth century? We still celebrate His birth at Christmastime, but actually who is He and why did He come?

IDENTIFICATION

The Gospel according to John introduces Him with three tremendous statements.

In the beginning was the Word
And the Word was with God
And the Word was God

"The Word" is one of the highest and most profound titles of the Lord Jesus Christ. To determine the exact meaning is not easy. Obviously the Lord Jesus Christ is not the *logos* of Greek philosophy, rather He is the *memra* of the Hebrew Scriptures.

Notice how important the Word is in the Old Testament. For instance, the name for Jehovah was never pronounced. It was such a holy word that they never used it at all. But this is the One who is the Word; and gathering up everything that was said of Him in the Old Testament, He is now presented as the One "in the beginning." This beginning antedates the very first words in the Bible, "In the beginning God created the heaven and the earth." That beginning can be dated, although I do not believe that anyone can date it accurately. It is nonsense to say that it is 4004 B.C., as Ussher's dating has it. It probably goes back billions and billions of years. You see, you and I are dealing with the God of eternity. When you go back to creation He is already there, and that is exactly the way this is used— "in the beginning *was* the Word." Notice it is not *is* the Word; it was not in the beginning that the Word started out or was begotten. *Was* (as Dr. Lenske points out) is known as a durative imperfect, meaning continued action. It means that the Word was in the beginning. What beginning? Just as far back as you want to go. The Bible says, "In the beginning God created the heaven and the earth." Does that begin God? No, just keep on going back billions and trillions and "squillions" of years. I can think back to billions of years before creation. Maybe you can go beyond that, but let's put down a point there, billions of years prior to creation. He already was; He comes out of eternity to meet us. He did not begin. "In the beginning *was* the Word"—He was already there when the beginning was.

"Well," somebody says, "there has to be a beginning somewhere." All right, wherever you begin, He is there to meet you, He is already past tense. "In the beginning was the Word"—five words in the original language, and there is not a man on topside of this earth who can put a date on it or understand it or fathom it. This first tremendous statement starts us off in space, you see.

The second statement is this, "And the Word was with God." This makes it abundantly clear that He is separate and distinct from God the Father. You cannot identify Him as God the Father because He is *with* God. "But," someone says, "if He is with God, He is not God." The third statement sets us straight, "And the Word was God." This is a clear, emphatic declaration that the Lord Jesus Christ is God. In fact, the Greek is more specific than this, because in the Greek language the important word is placed at the beginning of the sentence and it reads, "God was the Word." That is emphatic; you cannot get it more emphatic than that. Do you want to get rid of the deity of Christ? My friend, you cannot get rid of it. The first three statements in John's Gospel tie the thing down.

In the beginning was the Word, and the Word was with God, and the Word was God. (John 1:1)

INTERPRETATION

Let's move on down to verse 14 and notice the three statements there:

And the Word was made flesh
And the Word dwelt among us
He was full of grace and truth

The Greek philosopher probably would have stayed with us through verse one, but he leaves us here. He would never agree that the Word was made flesh. The Greek language allows us to put it more specifically and, I think, more accurately, "The Word was *born* flesh." Turn this over in your mind for a moment. Here comes God out of eternity, already the Ancient of days; but He also came to Bethlehem, a little baby thing that made a woman cry. And notice that John's Gospel does not even mention His birth in Bethlehem. Do you know why? He is talking about One who is too big for Bethlehem. Out of eternity, the Word became flesh.

"And [the Word] dwelt among us" is the second statement in John 1:14. "Dwelt" is from *skenoo;* it means He pitched His tent among us. Our human bodies are merely little tents in which we live. The apostle Paul used the same imagery, "We know that if our earthly house of this tabernacle were dissolved . . ." (2 Corinthians 5:1). This house in which we live is a tabernacle, a tent, that can be blown over in a night; it can be snuffed out in an instant. Because you and I live in these little tents, the God of eternity took upon Himself a human body and thus pitched His tent down here among us. Such is the second tremendous statement.

Notice the third, "And we beheld his glory, the glory as of the only begotten of the Father, full of grace and truth." Now John is saying something else. The observation I would naturally make at this point is, "If He was made flesh, He certainly limited Himself." John says, "Wait a minute. He was full of grace and truth." The word *full* means that you just could not have any more. He brought all the deity with Him, and He was full of grace and full of truth when He came down here.

ILLUMINATION

Now we move to verse eighteen to find three statements again:

No man hath seen God at any time
The only begotten Son, which is
in the bosom of the Father
He hath declared him

Notice the first, "No man hath seen God at any time." Why? He will explain it in this Gospel. The Lord Jesus will tell the woman at the well, "God is a Spirit: and they that worship him must worship him in spirit and in truth"—for God is spirit. No man has seen God at any time. What about the appearances in the Old Testament? God never revealed Himself in the Old Testament to the eyes of man. What, then, did they see? Well, go back and read the record. For instance, Jacob said that he saw God, but what he saw was the angel of the Lord who wrestled with him. That was a manifestation, but he did not see God, because God is a spirit. "No man hath seen God at any time."

The second statement is, "The only begotten Son. . . ." The best Greek text is that of Nestle, the German scholar. He has come to the definite conclusion that it is not the only begotten Son, but the only begotten *God*. I prefer that also. ". . . Which is in the bosom of the Father" tells us a great deal. He did not come from the head of God to reveal the wisdom of God; He did not come from the foot of God to be a servant of man. (Have you ever noticed this? Although we speak of the fact that He was a servant, whose shoes did He ever shine? Did He ever run an errand for anybody? He did not. He said, "I came down from heaven, not to do mine own will but the will of Him that sent Me." He was God's servant. He came to serve Him, and as He served the Father, He served men.) He did not come from the foot; He did not come from the head; it was from the bosom of the Father that He came. He came to reveal the heart of God. He was "the only begotten Son, which is in the bosom of the Father."

The third statement completes verse eighteen, "He hath declared him." The Greek word here is *exegesato*. *Ago* is "to lead" and *ex* is "out." It means that what Jesus Christ did was to lead God out into the open. Do you know anything bigger than that? A little trip to the moon is nothing in comparison. Here He comes out of eternity past, the God of this universe, the Creator of everything, taking upon Himself human flesh and bringing God out into the open so that men can know Him. My friend, the only way in the world you can know God is through this One, Jesus Christ. Jesus Christ came to reveal God because He is God.

I am not through with these statements; there is something else here. Let's put together the first verse in each of these three groups and see what we come up with:

> *In the beginning was the Word* (verse 1)
> *And the Word was made flesh* (verse 14)
> *No man hath seen God at any time* (verse 18)

You could not see God; God is spirit. He had to become flesh; He had to become one of us in order for us to know Him. We could not go up there to understand Him; He had to come down here and bring God down where we are.

Now let's put the second statements together from each of the three groups:

> *The Word was with God* (verse 1)
> *And dwelt among us* (verse 14)

The only begotten Son,
which is in the bosom of the Father (verse 18)

Consider this One for a moment—the angels bowed before Him; He was with God, on an equality with God. The apostle Paul wrote of Him, that He "thought it not robbery to be equal with God" (Philippians 2:6). That is, He did not go to school to become God, it was not something He worked overtime to attain. It was not a degree that He earned. He did not *try* to be God; He *was* God. I do not mean to be irreverent, but He did not say to the Father when He came to this earth, "Keep Your eye on Gabriel; he is after My job—watch him while I'm gone." He did not have to do that; nobody could take His place. He was God. Here He comes, born in Bethlehem, a few little shepherds there, not many; He goes up to Nazareth; for thirty years He is hidden away in Nazareth. God, out of eternity, comes down and goes to Nazareth, working in a carpenter shop. Why? So you can know God. The only way you will ever know Him, my friend, is to know this One. "The only begotten Son, which is in the bosom of the Father," He is the only One who can reveal God to us.

Now notice the third statement in each group:

The Word was God
And we beheld his glory, the glory as of the only
begotten of the Father, full of grace and truth
He hath declared him

When He was down here, He was still God, full of grace and truth. And He declared Him; He is the only One who can lead Him out in the open where we can get acquainted with Him.

We are not through with this. I want you to see something else. How do you divide up this universe? I sat with a man who designed the shield that has been on all these spacecrafts to make their re-entry. He is a scientist who is an authority on heat. As we had lunch together in New Jersey, he said, "You know, this universe is made up of just three things. I believe that God has put His fingerprints on everything—the Trinity is everywhere." Then he explained what he meant. The universe is divided up into time, space, and matter. Can you think of a fourth? The very interesting thing is that time, space, and matter include everything that is in this universe as you and I know it. Then time can be divided into just three parts: past, present, and future. Can you think of a fourth? And what about space? Length, breadth, and height. Is there another direction? Also in matter there is energy, motion, and phenomena. Those are the three divisions of the the three divisions. The universe in which we live bears the mark of the Trinity.

Now notice the way in which the Incarnation is geared into this observation.

Time: "In the beginning was the Word, and the Word was with God."

Space: "The Word was made flesh"—became flesh, came down into space. Where? To Bethlehem, a little geographical spot—and even this earth was a pretty small spot for Him to come to—and He pitched His tent here among us, we beheld His glory, full of grace and truth.

Matter: "No man hath seen God at any time; the only begotten Son which is in the bosom of the Father, he hath declared him." Because He became matter, became a man, took upon Himself humanity, men could see and know God. This is the time, space and matter of the Incarnation.

Let's divide each of these into three. First, let's look at time.

Past: "In the beginning *was* the Word."

Present: "The Word became flesh" (in our day).

Future: "No man hath seen God at any time; the only begotten Son . . . hath declared him." The apostle Paul, at the end of his life, said, "That I may know him, and the power of his resurrection . . ." (Philippians 3:10). That will be for the future—to really know Him; today we actually know so little because we are finite.

Then look at space, divided into length, breadth and height:

Length: "In the beginning was the Word."

Breadth: He came down to this earth and was made flesh.

Height: No man has seen God at any time. The only begotten Son, who is in the bosom of the Father, He has come from the heights to set Him before us.

Consider the divisions of matter: energy, motion and phenomena.

Energy: "In the beginning was the *Word,* and the *Word* was with God"—that's energy. How did this universe come into existence? God spoke. Every rational person has to confront this problem of how the universe began. That is the reason evolution has been popular—it offers to the natural man an explanation for the origin of the universe. You must have an explanation for it, if you do any thinking at all. Where did it come from? Well, here is the answer, "In the beginning was the Word." God spoke. That is the first thing that happened. When God speaks, when the Word speaks, energy is translated into matter. What is atomic fission? It is matter translated back into energy— poof! it disappears. Creation began with energy. In the beginning was the Word. The Word was with God, the Word was God.

Motion: The Word was made flesh. He came out of heaven's glory, and He came to this earth.

Phenomenon: The greatest phenomenon in this world is Jesus Christ. The wonders of the ancient world and the wonders we see in our day are nothing in comparison to the wonder of the Incarnation—God became man!

These statements are bigger than any of us, and yet they are so simple. We have read them, probably memorized them, yet no man can plumb the depths of them.

In the beginning was the Word, and the Word was with God, and the Word was God. . . . And the Word was made flesh, and dwelt among us, (and we beheld his glory, the glory as of the only begotten of the Father,) full of grace and truth. . . . No man hath seen God at any time; the only begotten Son, which is in the bosom of the Father, he hath declared him. (John 1:1, 14, 18)

These three verses are the great building blocks. Now let us consider some of the cement that holds them together.

All things were made by him; and without him was not any thing made that was made. (John 1:3)

The Lord Jesus Christ is the Creator. Not only did He exist before Bethlehem, but He created the vast universe, including the material out of which man constructed Bethlehem. All things were made by Him. He is the instrument of creation. Nothing came into existence without Him.

In him was life; and the life was the light of men. (John 1:4)

Now we are confronted with something else—two of the simplest things in the world: light and life. *Zoe* and *phos* are the two words in the original language. From *zoe* we get zoology, the study of life; and from *phos* we get photo or anything that is built on it, such as photograph—it is light. These two things are so common that we take them for granted. Life—we see it everywhere. There may be a great deal of life right where you are at this moment. You go out in the woods and you see the same thing—life. It greets you on every hand; but can you explain it? You see in the Sunday pictorials and the sensational magazines that men now have discovered the source of life. But if you read them, you find that they have not found the source at all, though they think they are close to it. They put the microscope down on a green leaf. One moment that little cell is arranged one way and is dead as a doornail. The next moment the thing is rearranged in another way and it is alive. And then the thing starts growing and doubling, dividing and multiplying itself. Why does it do that? Life.

The other common thing is light. What is light? I listened to Irwin Moon try to explain it (and Irwin gave the best explanation I have heard), but when he got through I was not sure if light is a real something or if it is just waves, because they can cut the thing off and still light will go through objects that would stop waves. What in the world is light?

You see, we are dealing with things that are fundamental, though men today, with all their scientific gadgets, know so little about them.

"In him was life"—all life is in Jesus Christ. "In him was life; and the life was the light of men." You and I live in a universe that is spiritually dark. The fact of the matter is that it is physically dark to a certain degree. But God said, "Let there be light," and these light holders are placed about throughout His universe like street lights in a big city. We are told that when a man gets away from this earth a short distance, he is in total, absolute darkness, and it is frightening to be out where there is nothing from which the sun can be reflected. Our little globe is out in a dark universe, yet that is nothing compared to the spiritual darkness that envelops it. When the sun disappears, there is physical darkness over the land; but twenty-four hours a day there is spiritual darkness here, awful spiritual darkness. Man does not know God; man is in rebellion against God; man is in sin that blinds him to God. In the Lord Jesus Christ there is life, and the life that He gives is the *light* of men. In fact, His life is the only thing that can kindle light in the heart of an individual. An unregenerate man has no spiritual life within him. This is the reason that when you present to him Jesus Christ, he says, "I don't get it. I don't understand that at all."

I used to go down to the jail in Cleburne, Texas, and

speak to the men. It was not a large jail and I could talk to them in a conversational tone. I would start off talking about football (because in Texas football is a religion!) and those hardened men would get enthusiastic about it. I talked also of other things, and they were interested. Then I would turn the conversation to something spiritual, and I could see the darkness come over their faces. I might just as well have been talking to corpses. And that is what they were—men dead in trespasses and sins. This world today is in spiritual darkness, and the Lord Jesus Christ has brought the only light there is in the world. He is the light.

In him was life; and the life was the light of men. And the light shineth in darkness; and the darkness comprehended it not (John 1:4–5)

DARKNESS OF DOUBT

The light shines in the darkness of this world at this moment. I have a notion that somebody reading these pages is saying, "Why is that preacher talking about being in spiritual darkness? I understand everything." No, unless you know Jesus Christ as your Savior, you do not understand. The Spirit of God has to open your heart and mind and enlighten you before you can ever see Him as your Savior and receive Him as your own. May I say to you, friend, this world is in spiritual darkness.

The light shineth in darkness; and the darkness comprehended it not. (John 1:5)

That word *comprehend* is an unfortunate translation. And a wiseacre did not help it by rendering it, "and the darkness was not able to put it out." That is no translation at all. The word in the Greek is *katelaben,* meaning actually "to take down." It is the picture of a secretary to whom the boss is giving dictation, and she stops and says, "I can't take that down; I am not able to take it down." The light shines in darkness, and the darkness is not able to take it in. That is it exactly. Someone said to me, "Boy, was I in darkness before I received Christ! And I don't know why I didn't see." Well, that is it, you were in darkness and you did not see. The darkness just cannot take it in.

Now this is something quite interesting, and it is not true of physical light. You go into a dark room, and the minute you switch on the light, the darkness leaves, it disappears. Darkness and light cannot exist together physically. The moment you bring light in, darkness is gone. The minute light is taken out, darkness will come right back in. But *spiritual* light and darkness exist together. Sometimes here is a husband who is saved and a wife who is unsaved—or vice versa. Here is a man working next to another man. He says, "What do you mean when you talk about being a Christian? I do the best I can. Am I not a Christian?" There you have light and darkness side by side, and the darkness just cannot take it in. That is exactly what is said here, "The light shineth in darkness; and the darkness comprehended it not."

He was in the world, and the world was made by him, and the world knew him not. (John 1:10)

That was the tragedy—the world was in darkness, spiritual darkness, and did not know Him. Even today we are seeing the rise of atheism and unbelief and will see it more and more in the days ahead. A great many people do not seem to recognize that unbelief and atheism go naturally with the natural man. Somebody says to me, "Oh, did you read in the paper what Dr. So-and-so of a certain seminary wrote?" Yes, I read it. "Well, isn't it awful?" No, I do not think so. He would upset my apple cart if he said that he believed the Bible, because he is an unbeliever by his own statement. He says that he does not believe in being born again, that he does not believe he has to receive Christ in order to be saved. Now I do not expect that man to say he believes the Bible. That would be absolutely contrary to his statements. The so-called theologians and theological professors who espouse the "God is dead movement" present us with the preposterous, untenable claim that they are Christian atheists! Obviously atheism precludes the possibility of being Christian, yet unbelief has moved into our seminaries and pulpits across the land. The world does not know Him.

He was in the world, and the world was made by him, and the world knew him not. He came unto his own [his own things], *and his own* [people] *received him not.* (John 1:10–11).

He came into His own universe, but His own people did not receive Him.

DEEPEST NEED

"But as many as received him, to them gave he power. . . ." The word "power" is not *dunamis* power like dynamite, physical power, but *exousian* power which is delegated power, authority.

But as many as received him, to them gave he power [the authority] *to become the sons of God* [children, *tekna* of God], *even to them that believe on his name.* (John 1:12)

This week I looked over the shoulder of a person who was reading an out-of-town paper (that's a Scotchman's way of reading newspapers) and I saw where an outstanding columnist, writing about this present-day spree of trying to get peace by going to a psychologist and by using tranquilizers, made the statement that until men find peace in God they will never know what real peace is.

Notice that this is for "them that *believe* on his name."

And always with the word "believe" there is a preposition.
You see, faith, as the Bible uses it, is not just head knowledge. Many people ask, "You mean all that I have to do is
to say I believe?" Yes, that is all you have to do, but let's see
what that implies. With the verb *to believe* there is always a
preposition—sometimes *en* (in), sometimes *eis* (into) or
sometimes *epi* (upon). You must believe into, in, or upon
Jesus Christ. Let me illustrate with a chair. I am standing
beside a chair and I believe it will hold me up, but it is not
holding me up. Why? Because I have only a head knowledge. I just say, "Yes, it will hold me up." Now suppose I
believe into the chair by sitting in it. See what I mean? I am
committing my entire weight to it, and it is holding me up.
Is Christ holding you up? Is He your Savior? It is not a
question of standing to the side and saying, "Oh, yes, I
believe Jesus is the Son of God." The question is, have you
trusted Him, have you believed into Him, are you resting
in Him? This chair is holding me up completely. And at
this moment Christ is my complete Savior. I am depending
on Him; I am resting in Him.

In the state of Mississippi, back in the antebellum days, a
slave preacher was speaking to the other slaves at the close
of the day. They were tired and weary and were reclining
on their cotton sacks at the end of the cotton rows. He
quoted to them, "Come unto me, all ye that labor and are
heavy laden, and I will rest you." One of the men raised up
from his cotton sack and said, "Preacher, them's good
words, but who said them?"

That, my friend, is the most profound question that can
be asked. "Who said them?" And that question, voiced
long ago in a cotton field in the South, is the same question
in the mind of modern man, weary of the pressures and
frustrations of life.

*Come unto me, all ye that labour and are heavy laden,
and I will give you rest.* (Matthew 11:28)

"Them's good words, but who said them?" Who said them? Jesus, the Word, God become man.

I ask you the question: Who is Jesus? Do you have some question about Him? If you do, there is no peace in your heart. But if by faith you can accept God's record—the Word came out of eternity, was made flesh, walked these dusty roads down here, went to a cross, died as man's substitute, and arose from the dead to be an adequate Savior—if you can believe this, you not only will be God's child for eternity, but you will have rest, the peace of God in your heart right now. You will have a Savior who is too big for Bethlehem, who is bigger than this world, who is adequate to meet your need. I present Him to you today as Jesus, the Savior of the world.

─6─

HE IS COMING AGAIN!

(John 14:3)

In World War II when General Douglas MacArthur withdrew from the Philippines—after Pearl Harbor and before the surrender of Corregidor—he issued his now famous statement: "I will return." For several years millions of people in the Orient hung onto these three words as the only ray of light in the darkness of tyranny and oppression. They were words of hope; they were words of promised deliverance for people around the world.

MacArthur did return. He returned with a vengeance. Not stopping at Manila, he went on to Tokyo to receive the surrender of the proud nation of Japan on the deck of the battleship *Missouri*. Although he was, after all, a frail human being, he kept his promise. He did return.

Before the Lord Jesus Christ left this earth to return to heaven, He said, "I will come again." These words have been the hope and comfort of millions of believers for the past twenty centuries. He, as the glorified Christ, repeated these words to the apostle John on the lonely island of Patmos. Here He sharpened His promise and delivered it in a dramatic way, "And, behold, I come quickly; and my reward is with me" (Revelation 22:12). He did not mean that He was coming *soon*—that is not what He said. He said that His coming, with all that it entailed, would oc-

cupy a very brief time—"I come *quickly*." The book of
Revelation closes the Bible with His affirmation, "He
which testifieth these things saith, Surely I come quickly.
Amen." This is the last promise that has come to us from
heaven. "I come quickly." And these words have been the
comfort of His own for twenty centuries.

It is the thought of some that the Revelation is a book
filled only with that which is frightful and sensational.
There are symbols of wild beasts, monstrous creatures;
there are convulsions of nature, thunders and lightnings
and earthquakes; there are trumpets of judgment and
bowls of wrath. But all of these are incidental. They are the
freaks one sees in the sideshow. The main event is the
return to this earth of Jesus Christ. Christ's return is the
central truth, the primary meaning of this book. The pre-
vailing purpose of Revelation is to say just one thing: "I will
come again."

The book of the Revelation opens with the statement:
"The Revelation of Jesus Christ." The word "revelation"
comes from the Latin *revelatio,* an unveiling. The Greek
word is *apokalupsis,* the removing of a veil. By translitera-
tion *apokalupsis* is our word "apocalypse." The Revelation
is the apocalypse or the unveiling of Jesus Christ.

At Christ's first coming He was not revealed—rather He
was concealed. "The Word was made flesh, and dwelt
among us," says John 1:14. The Word (Christ) was made
flesh and took upon Himself the tabernacle or the tent of
flesh. Just as God had manifested Himself back in the Old
Testament through a tabernacle with all sorts of coverings
and curtains that shut man out from Him, so the Lord
Jesus came in a tabernacle of flesh. He was put in the con-
cealing wraps of a human body. God was not revealed
when Christ came the first time. It still can be said, "No
man hath seen God at any time; the only begotten Son,
which is in the bosom of the Father, he hath declared him"
(John 1:18). Christ, when He came, declared God; He ex-
egeted Him, let Him out in the open where, for the first

time, one can see the heart of God. Yet we have not seen *God.* The first coming of Christ was not the revelation of Jesus Christ. The revelation of Jesus Christ takes place at His second coming. Actually the first and second comings of Christ are component parts of a whole.

At His first coming the great word was *grace.* He came that men might experience something of the grace of God. When He comes the second time, the preeminent word will be *glory.* Men will see for the first time the glory of God. When He came the first time He was veiled in human flesh; when He comes the second time the veil will be removed and every eye shall see Him. For the first time men will see God!

Since the first and second comings of Christ belong together, we shall place them together. First we shall consider the *contrasts* between the first and second comings of Christ, then a comparison of the two comings, and finally the completion—the second coming of Christ completing His first coming.

CONTRAST

Let us see the first and second comings of Christ in contrast. Listen to the writer to the Hebrews:

> *So Christ was once offered to bear the sins of many; and unto them that look for him shall he appear the second time without sin unto salvation.* (Hebrews 9:28)

When Christ came the first time it was to settle one question and one alone—the question of sin. He did not come to solve the problems of government nor to set before the world a philosophy of living. He came the first time to settle the sin question, to die for the sins of the world. When He comes the second time He will solve the governmental problems, the political and social dilemmas that harass our world. But up to this moment He deals only with the issue of sin in your heart and in mine. This is the preeminent contrast between the first and second comings of Christ.

It is interesting to note that the Scriptures make the contrast very sharp. He came the first time riding on a little donkey. He will come the second time riding a white charger. The first time He came to an out-of-the-way place, riding on a common beast of burden, in the womb of a woman! I challenge you to show how God could have humbled Himself more completely. The first time He came as Savior. The second time He will come as Sovereign. He will come in devastating majesty—listen to John describe it:

> *I saw heaven opened, and behold a white horse; and he that sat upon him was called Faithful and True, and in righteousness he doth judge and make war.* (Revelation 19:11)

Coming the first time in weakness, in meekness, in obscurity, He will come the next time in power to assert His will over all the earth; and before Him every knee shall bow!

When He came the first time the door of the inn was shut in His face, slamming so loudly that after about two thousand years it still can be heard. My friend, He is being shut out today. Even during the Christmas season which commemorates His birth, He is shut out. Oh, the cash registers ring so loudly that you may not hear the slamming of the door, but it is slamming, shutting Him outside. However, for His second coming we read of a door opened in heaven out of which He rides as *King of kings and Lord of lords*. The first time the door of the inn was closed; the second time the door of heaven will open. What a contrast!

His coming was shrouded in secret. Very few knew when He came the first time. When Jerusalem closed its shops that Christmas Eve it did not know what was taking place, and it cared less. Even Bethlehem did not know. Today the whole world knows when a head of state visits another country, but the whole world did not know that the Son of God came to Bethlehem, and it does not know it after all these years!

God had said that His birth, His life and His death should be characterized by lowliness. Isaiah put it this way:

> *And there shall come forth a rod out of the stem of Jesse, and a Branch shall grow out of his roots. (Isaiah 11:1)*

Why did Isaiah, who repeatedly mentioned the fact that Christ was the Branch of David, say in this instance that He was the Branch of *Jesse?* The reason is obvious when you look closely at Mary and Joseph. Jesse, the father of King David, was a peasant. When Jesus came, the royal line of David had been reduced again to peasantry, and Jesus comes as a Branch of Jesse, the peasant. Listen to Isaiah as God speaks of His life:

> *Behold my servant, whom I uphold; mine elect, in whom my soul delighteth; I have put my spirit upon him; he shall bring forth judgment to the Gentiles.* (Isaiah 42:1)

But before He comes in judgment:

> *He shall not cry, nor lift up, nor cause his voice to be heard in the street. A bruised reed shall he not break, and the smoking flax shall he not quench: he shall bring forth judgment unto truth.* (Isaiah 42:2–3)

Of His death He writes:

> *He is despised and rejected of men; a man of sorrows, and acquainted with grief: and we hid as it were our faces from him; he was despised, and we esteemed him not.* (Isaiah 53:3)

These Scriptures were ignored by the scribes in Jesus' day —which is the reason they did not believe the wise men who said, "Where is he that is born King of the Jews? for we have seen his star in the east, and are come to worship him" (Matthew 2:2). The scribes answered in effect, "The prophecy is that Christ will be born in Bethlehem, but anybody knows He is not down there now. The newspaper reporters are not there; the photographers are not there. No deliverer has arisen in Bethlehem. We know He has not come" (see Matthew 2). They were wrong because they had ignored the Scriptures that spoke of His lowliness.

> *They all were looking for a King*
> *To slay their foes and lift them high:*
> *Thou cam'st, a little baby thing*
> *That made a woman cry.*
>
> —George Macdonald

Yet let us not be too harsh with them for being dubious and not going with the wise men to worship Him. You see, they had other Scriptures that led them to believe that He was coming as a king in great power and glory.

> **Who is this that cometh from Edom, with dyed garments from Bozrah? this that is glorious in his apparel, travelling in the greatness of his strength? I that speak in righteousness, mighty to save.** (Isaiah 63:1)

He is coming in glory here! Daniel also saw a glorious coming:

> *I saw in the night visions, and, behold, one like the Son of man came with the clouds of heaven, and came to the Ancient of days, and they brought him near before him. And there was given him dominion, and glory, and a kingdom, that all people, nations, and languages, should serve him: his dominion is an everlasting do-*

minion, which shall not pass away, and his kingdom that which shall not be destroyed. (Daniel 7:13–14)

Hear Malachi:

Behold, I will send my messenger, and he shall prepare the way before me: and the Lord, whom ye seek, shall suddenly come to his temple, even the messenger of the covenant, whom ye delight in: behold, he shall come, saith the LORD of hosts. But who may abide the day of his coming? and who shall stand when he appeareth? for he is like a refiner's fire, and like fullers' soap. (Malachi 3:1–2)

Such Scriptures could be multiplied again and again in the Old Testament. And when you come to the conclusion of the New Testament where John looks forward to His coming again, we read:

Behold, he cometh with clouds; and every eye shall see him, and they also which pierced him: and all kindreds of the earth shall wail because of him. (Revelation 1:7)

That is His second coming.

What a contrast between the first and second comings of Christ!

COMPARISON

Now notice with me a comparison of the first and second comings of Christ. The second coming of Christ is in two phases, it is a drama of two acts. The first is what we please to call the "Rapture." Christ Himself was the first to speak of it. You will find no reference to it until you come to the fourteenth chapter of John's Gospel, where He tells of taking people off this earth up to a place which He is going to prepare. To His own He said:

In my Father's house are many mansions: if it were not so, I would have told you. I go to prepare a place for you. And if I go and prepare a place for you, I will come again, and receive you unto myself; that where I am, there ye may be also. (John 14:2–3)

This is the first phase of His second coming. But Christ spoke also of His coming to establish His kingdom upon this earth in power and glory. When He was brought before the high priest at His trial, He was put on oath, "Art thou the Christ, the Son of the Blessed?" Listen to His reply:

And Jesus said, I am: and ye shall see the Son of man sitting on the right hand of power, and coming in the clouds of heaven. (Mark 14:62)

Thus we see that Christ Himself spoke of both phases of His coming again.

The first phase of the second coming of Christ is to believers "that blessed hope and glorious appearing of our great God and Savior." There is nothing between us and that—no Great Tribulation, no other event that must take place. He could come today, but we do not say that He will, for we do not know. But we today are not looking for the Antichrist; we are looking for Christ Himself!

For the Lord himself shall descend from heaven with a shout, with the voice of the archangel, and with the trump of God: and the dead in Christ shall rise first: then we which are alive and remain shall be caught up together with them in the clouds, to meet the Lord in the air: and so shall we ever be with the Lord. (1 Thessalonians 4:16–17)

After our "gathering together unto Him," the second phase of the second coming of Christ will come upon the earth. It will begin with a time of great trouble. The world is moving into it at this moment. Just as a boat moves into a tornado or a typhoon at sea, our world is moving into this time of trouble. Christ said that it will be a short interval which will be blocked off by catastrophes "such as was not since the beginning of the world to this time, no, nor ever shall be." Nothing like it has taken place before, and nothing like it will ever take place afterward. It is His judgment, the Great Tribulation, described for us in terrible detail in the book of the Revelation. It will be climaxed by His personal return, His catastrophic and cataclysmic coming in glory to establish His kingdom by putting down all unrighteousness. Christ Himself shall sit upon the throne of David and shall rule on this physical earth.

Our critics today cynically and dubiously say, "Well, you really believe in a second and third coming of Christ." Oh, no. Let us make a comparison. When He came the first time there was a birth, which we commemorate at the Christmas season. It was the prophet Micah who wrote:

> *But thou, Bethlehem Ephratah, though thou be little among the thousands of Judah, yet out of thee shall he come forth unto me that is to be ruler in Israel; whose goings forth have been from of old, from everlasting.* (Micah 5:2)

This concerned the birth of Christ. But I also read of Him in Psalm 22:1,16–18:

> *My God, my God, why hast thou forsaken me? . . . The assembly of the wicked have inclosed me: they pierced my hands and my feet. I may tell [count] all my bones: they look and stare upon me. They part my garments among them, and cast lots upon my vesture.*

Clearly these verses speak of His death. Both of these events, His birth and His death, are included in His first coming—yet they are thirty-three years apart. Even so, His coming in the air to take believers, both living and dead, out of this earth and His coming to the earth as King is all called His second coming, although these two events are separated by at least seven years. When the comparison is made with that which has already taken place, it is easily seen.

COMPLETION

Finally let us consider the first and second comings of Christ as to the completion. The second coming of Christ is the completion of His first coming. He must come again to complete the work of His first coming. "But," you may say, "He said on the cross, 'It is finished.' " Yes, the work of redemption was finished. He had wrought out for you and me a way of salvation. As Paul very definitely says, "For other foundation can no man lay than that is laid, which is Jesus Christ" (1 Corinthians 3:11). He put down the foundation for your salvation and mine. But the towers have not yet been put on. He has not yet completed His work of salvation. He won only a partial victory when He came the first time. It was a truncated triumph. Although He won the battle, He did not receive the booty. He gained the victory, but He did not receive the kingdom.

Actually salvation is in three tenses. I can say that I *have been* saved, I can also say I *am being* saved, and I can say I *shall be* saved. All three are true. I *have been* saved—"He that heareth my word, and believeth on him that sent me, hath everlasting life" (John 5:24). I have right here and now eternal life. The moment we trust Christ, receiving God's gift of eternal life, we are as much saved as we will be a billion years from today—complete in Him, saved in Him. Also I *am being* saved—there needs to be a work within. Paul could say to the Philippian Christians, ". . . Work out your own salvation with fear and trembling. For it is God which worketh in you both to will and to do of his good pleasure" (Philippians 2:12–13). We ought to be patient with one another. There are a few people who are very critical of this preacher. Be a little more patient with me—God is not through with me. Someday I *shall be* saved; someday I shall be like Him.

> *Beloved, now are we the sons of God, and it doth not yet appear what we shall be: but we know that, when he shall appear, we shall be like him; for we shall see him as he is.* (1 John 3:2)

He began the work about two thousand years ago when He took upon Himself the likeness of sinful flesh (yet without sin) in order that in time He might present you and me in His own likeness. That is going to be a wonderful day, the day when you and I will be like Jesus! Let us be patient with one another. Though we are now the sons of God, it does not yet appear what we shall be. Paul writes to the Roman Christians:

> *For I reckon that the sufferings of this present time are not worthy to be compared with the glory which shall be revealed in us. For the earnest expectation of the creature waiteth for the manifestation of the sons of God. . . . And not only they, but ourselves also, which have the firstfruits of the Spirit, even we ourselves groan within ourselves, waiting for the adoption, to wit, the redemption of our body.* (Romans 8:18–19, 23)

A great day is coming!

And we have a redeemed body coming up in the future. It will be a body that will not have pain or disease or weakness, nor will it be subject to all the limitations of this life. We hear some say that healing is in the atonement. So is a new body! But we do not have it yet. The package He gives is labeled "Do not open until Christmas." The error of the folk who are involved in these healing movements is that they are trying to open their packages before Christmas. The redemption of the body is in the future. One of these days we shall receive a new body. What a gift that will be!

That is not all we will get. Look again at the eighth chapter of Romans:

> *For the creature was made subject to vanity, not willingly, but by reason of him who hath subjected the same in hope. Because the creature itself also shall be delivered from the bondage of corruption into the glorious liberty of the children of God. For we know that the whole creation groaneth and travaileth in pain together until now.* (Romans 8:20–22)

The human family is trying to be happy. Yet there are many broken hearts; the hospitals are crowded; the cemeteries are being filled; even nature itself is groaning. You go down to the seaside and you can hear the sob of the waves; you go to the mountains and you can hear the low sigh of the wind in the treetops Creation is groaning, waiting for the glorious day when Christ shall return and lift the curse. Then the package will explode into a new heaven and a new earth!

> *And I saw a new heaven and a new earth: for the first heaven and the first earth were passed away; and there was no more sea. . . . And I heard a great voice out of heaven saying, Behold, the tabernacle of God is with men, and he will dwell with them, and they shall be his people, and God himself shall be with them, and be their God. And God shall wipe away all tears from their eyes; and there shall be no more death, neither sorrow, nor crying, neither shall there be any more pain: for the former things are passed away.* (Revelation 21:1, 3–4)

What a glorious day that will be!

Someone may be thinking, *I would like to have a stake in this which is coming. I would like to have part in that day of the future.* You may. The vital thing is to be properly related to Jesus Christ. Christianity is not a religion; it is a relationship—a personal relationship to Jesus Christ. The gift of God is eternal life in Christ Jesus. This can be yours.

How do you get a gift? I am wearing a watch that was given to me twenty years ago. It was handed to me in a little box with the words, "This is a gift." For twenty years I have never paid one penny for this watch. For twenty years it has been *my* watch because by simple faith I held out my hand and took it as a gift. God is holding out to this lost world a gift—eternal life in Christ Jesus. You may have it by receiving Christ in simple faith.

Christ came almost two thousand years ago to be your Savior.

He came unto his own, and his own received him not. But as many as received him, to them gave he power to become the sons of God, even to them that believe on his name. (John 1:11–12)

He came yesterday as the world's Savior. He will come tomorrow as the world's Sovereign. Almost two thousand years ago the Lord Jesus Christ said,

I will come again. (John 14:3)

Even so, come, Lord Jesus.

—7—

BEHIND THE BLACK CURTAIN IN THE UPPER ROOM

(John 13:33–14:27)

In the Upper Room our Lord began immediately to deal with those who were His own in a way He had never dealt with them or anyone else before. He began to talk about things He had never before talked about. He was attempting to lift their thinking to a high plane—because these men were frightened.

They knew something tremendous was in the offing and that they were facing a crisis. Yonder in the Upper Room sin was knocking at the door, demanding its pound of flesh. Also behind the black curtain in that Upper Room was the long, thin hand of death stretching forth to reach their Savior. These men were rightly frightened. They didn't know what to think as they looked at the circumstances around them. As they looked, our Lord attempted to lift their thinking from a low plane to a high plane. He attempted to take them from the here-and-now to the hereafter. He attempted to lift them from the physical to the spiritual. He attempted to take them from the things which were at their fingertips to the thing that was beyond what their eye could see or their ear could hear. He was drawing their thinking yonder, and that is where He would have us think today.

As our Lord moves along, He is interrupted. He is interrupted by four men who stand out in the crowd of eleven disciples. These four men have the spotlight put on them and the cameras trained on them for a moment as they speak out. They are attempting to stop Him and pull Him back because they have questions that are bothering them in a desperate sort of way. Our Lord in a patient manner answers the questions of these men and, in doing so, leads them to the very heights.

We want to follow Him as He moves up and out in that Upper Room.

The first thing that He said triggered all their interruptions. He said in substance, "I have been saying to the Jews on the outside that I am going to leave and they won't see Me. Now I want to say it to you. You are My disciples."

Little children, yet a little while I am with you. Ye shall seek me; and as I said unto the Jews, Where I go, ye cannot come; so now I say to you. (John 13:33)*

As He was telling them He was going to leave, He said in effect, "Now the brand I want to be on you is love, which will let the world know that you belong to Me."

By this shall all men know that ye are my disciples, if ye have love one to another. (John 13:35)

SIMON PETER

It was a wonderful discourse, but there was sitting there a disciple who missed it. He heard only one thing. He heard the Lord Jesus say that He was going away, that He was going to leave them. He held on to that. He is the first

---

* All Scripture references are from *The New Scofield Reference Bible.*

one to interrupt our Lord. He was, of course, Simon Peter. The first man in that crowd who *would* speak out would always be Simon Peter. He thought every occasion was an auspicious occasion to make a speech. Believe me, he was on his feet if there was ever an opportunity to say something. And he generally said the wrong thing. Although he reached spiritual maturation later on, here we see this robust fisherman that he was, nothing more than a child in his thinking and in his spiritual life.

This is not farfetched, because our Lord dealt with him that way. Notice that the Lord Jesus said, "I'm going away. And while I'm away I want you to exhibit to the world love for one another." Simon Peter didn't hear that—all he heard was that Jesus was going away. So at the first opportunity he broke in and said, "Lord, where goest Thou? You say You are going away? I'd like to know where You are going." My friend, that is the question of a child. You have seen a father put on his hat and his coat and start going out when his little son, who has been playing on the floor, jumps up and says, "Daddy, where are you going?" That is the question of a child. And every child asks that question. And childlike, Simon Peter will not sit by silently and let the Lord Jesus say, "I'm going away," without saying, "Where are You going? I want to know."

And the Lord Jesus dealt with him just as one deals with a child. Listen to Him:

> . . . *Jesus answered him, Where I go, thou canst not follow me now; but thou shalt follow me afterwards.*
> (John 13:36)

That's the way we answer a child, is it not? When little Willie comes in at five o'clock in the afternoon and says, "I want a piece of cake," Mama says, "Not now, but after supper." That's the way you deal with a child. Simon Peter says, "Where are You going? I want to know where You are going." The Lord Jesus says, "You can't follow Me now, but afterwards."

Simon Peter then raises the question, "Why cannot I follow Thee now?" Again he is the child. When the father puts on his coat and hat, the child says, "Where are you going, Daddy? I want to go with you." The father says, "You can't go with me now, but I'll take you afterwards." Simon Peter says, "Why can't I go with You *now?*" Peter was ready to go *now.* And the little child is ready to go too, my beloved. He'll go get his hat and coat, and he'll say, "I want to go *now,*" having no notion where the father is going. And Simon Peter, with no notion of where the Lord Jesus was going, said in substance, "Wherever You go I want to go with You. When I left that fishing boat the last time—and it took me a long time to give it up—I said I would go with You all the way. And I really meant it." He *did* mean it. Listen to him here, "I will lay down my life for Thy sake" (John 13:37).

Many Christians, when they stand on the threshold of the new year, will resolve in their hearts to live for Him in the year that lies ahead. They will say, "I failed You last year, but this year You can count on me." If you really want to know the truth, the Lord can't count on you. Neither can He count on me. If He would take His hand off me for five minutes, I'd deny Him.

Simon Peter said, "I'll follow You to death. I'll lay down my life for Your sake." And he was honest and sincere. He meant every word he said. I know he did because *I* said it, and *I* meant every word. You've said it and you have meant every word. But we had to eat those words later on, did we not?

Listen to our Lord as He deals with this man:

Jesus answered him, Wilt thou lay down thy life for my sake? Verily, verily, I say unto thee, The cock shall not crow, till thou hast denied me thrice. (John 13:38)

Simon Peter did not believe that, but several hours went by, and during those hours this man denied his Lord. Then he went out yonder and mingled his tears with the dew of the grass on the hillside. This man had made a discovery. He had found out how weak he really was. A great many Christians today do not know how weak they really are. They think they have within themselves a sufficiency to meet the crises of life. They do not know how much they need God in this hour in which they are living.

Now chapter divisions are wonderful to help all of us find our way around in the Scriptures, but sometimes they are in the wrong place. Do not make a break between chapters 13 and 14. Our Lord is continuing to talk to Simon Peter, which is the reason this section has meant so much to so many people—it was given to a man in the hour of his emergency, in the darkest time of his life. Our Lord, knowing that Peter would deny Him, was putting down a cushion for him.

> *Let not your heart be troubled; ye believe in God, believe also in me.* (John 14:1)

It was as though He said, "Simon Peter, tonight you will do the most dastardly deed any man will do—with the exception of Judas Iscariot, and your deed will be close to his —but I have prayed that your faith would not fail. You may have denied Me; I have not denied you. This night I do not want your heart to be troubled. You believe in God; believe also in Me. Although this night you will fail and hate yourself for it, you can come to Me."

Beloved, when we stand on the threshold of a new year, our Lord is saying to you and me—and it makes no difference who you are or what your failure is—"Let not *your* heart be troubled. I'll stick by you."

What a Savior! Not only did He reach down to save us those many years ago, but today He abides faithful.

Then He says,

In my Father's house are many mansions. . . .

The word "mansions" is an unfortunate translation here. The Greek word is *mone*, meaning "abiding places." In the Father's house are many abiding places. I do not know about you, but I do not want a mansion in heaven. I'll settle for a little California bungalow anytime.

This universe is so tremendous that astronomers have no notion of the number of stars; they have no notion what is the actual size of it. Our most up-to-date telescopes are not even good bifocals for seeing God's universe. It is my theory that in all of God's universe He doesn't have an apartment for rent anywhere. They are all occupied. God has, I think, created intelligences throughout His universe. Jesus says, "In My Father's house are many abiding places where My creatures are, but I am going to prepare a special place for you."

Now He says something that is brand new to them. It has become very familiar to us, but I hope it has not become commonplace because it is the great hope of the church. The future home of the believer is not here on this earth.

And if I go and prepare a place for you, I will come again, and receive you unto myself, that where I am, there ye may be also. (John 14:3)

Jesus says here that He is going to do something He never said in the Old Testament that He would do; that is, to take us out of this world that we might be with Him in the place He has prepared for us.

Among the many things our Lord is doing today is preparing abiding places for His own. I think He is still the Carpenter of Nazareth. He is preparing a place for His own. And He is saying this directly to a man who in the next few hours will deny Him. He says, "Though you will deny Me tonight, let not your heart be troubled because it won't in any way change My plans concerning you. I am going to prepare a place for you." My friend, if God has saved you and He doesn't get you to heaven, He'll have a house vacant throughout eternity because He has prepared a place for you. Jesus said, "I am coming again." This was a wonderful revelation to these men who had never heard anything like it before.

THOMAS

Sitting there in the Upper Room was a man who possibly was the greatest skeptic who has ever lived—that fellow Thomas. I don't know, but I do not think I would have called him as a disciple. Would you? As a matter of fact, I don't know that I would have called any one of these twelve men for disciples—I wouldn't want any one of them! I am glad that our Lord called them, though, because if He could use them, He may use me and He may use you.

He called Thomas, the doubter. He always was a doubter. The first time you see him he is doubting. He said to the other disciples, "Let's go with Him to Jerusalem and die with Him. This thing is getting serious." He had his doubts. It was gloom as far as he was concerned. And after the resurrection when Jesus appeared to the other disciples, Thomas, I think, was infuriated when these men said, "We have seen Him." I think that he said, "I heard the women say they had seen Him, but they're just a bunch of women. I thought you fellows had better sense than that. I want you to know that I don't believe in the resurrection, and I won't believe it until I put my finger in His wounds." This man was a doubter, he was a skeptic, he had a question mark for a brain. I know some folk like this—they question everything. The Lord has the answer for these folk too, as He had for Thomas.

After our Lord said, "And where I go ye know, and the way ye know," Thomas, this magnificent doubter, sitting there that night on the sidelines, said in substance, "Wait a minute. You say You are going to leave us and that we are going to be with You. You say we know where You are going and we know the way." Listen to him,

> *Thomas saith unto him, Lord, we know not where thou goest; and how can we know the way?* (John 14:5)

Today that question sounds like blasphemy. Questioning the Lord is something you ought not to do. But let me say to you that if you have a doubt, bring it out in the open to the Lord. Don't bury your doubts in a pious sort of way. Don't submerge your doubts and your questions and put on a pious front by saying, "I'm trusting the Lord," while you know good and well you're not trusting the Lord. If you doubt Him, don't publish your doubts, but take them to Him privately and tell Him that you have your doubts. No one yet has come to Him in this way without having his doubts resolved. The trouble with most doubters is that they are dishonest.

In college my philosophy professor doubted the Bible. He questioned everything. Finally his wife had him arrested for immorality. Of course he doubted the Bible! Any man who is living contrary to it will doubt it. He will want to get rid of it. But if you are honest and really have a doubt, bring it to Him like Thomas did.

Thomas says to Him, "You talk about going away. We don't know where You are going. How can we know the way?" I'm thankful that Thomas was there in the Upper Room because he elicited from the lips of our Lord this tremendous answer, the gospel in a nutshell:

> *Jesus saith unto him, I am the way, the truth, and the life; no man cometh unto the Father, but by me.* (John 14:6)

That answers once and for all the question of the way to God. Is the way to God through a church, a denomination?

Is the way to God through a ceremony? Is the way to God today a system of ethics? While I believe in the church, and I am not opposed to denominationalism; while I believe in a ceremony (I think it is essential to be baptized if you are a Christian); while I think that Christianity presents the highest system of ethics the world has ever seen, let's be clear on one fact: the way to God is through a Person and that Person is Christ. You either have Him or you don't have Him. You either trust Him or you don't trust Him. There is no such thing as middle ground. When Jesus said, "I am the way, the truth, and the life," He made a dead-end street of every other way, of every ism and every cult. Jesus Christ is the way to the Father.

When He said, "I am the way," He didn't mean that He was a way-shower. He said, "I *am* the way." He said, "I am the truth"—not I *tell* the truth (although He did tell the truth)—but I *am* the truth, I am the touchstone of truth, I am the bureau of standards of truth. Also He said, "I am the life," not the *source* of life.

That statement is dogmatic. Several years ago I was speaking at a Bible club at UCLA, using John 14:6. A young fellow came up to me afterwards and said, "Dr. McGee, I have one criticism of that verse. It is too dogmatic." I said to him, "I agree with you. It is dogmatic. In fact, it is the most dogmatic statement I can think of. But it is the characteristic of truth to be dogmatic." Then I gave him the illustration of a teacher I had when I was first starting out in school. She taught me that 2+2=4. She was not broad-minded about it. She had no tolerance for anything else. To be honest with you, I was very broad-minded in those days. As far as I was concerned 2+2 could equal 3 or 5. But she was very dogmatic. She insisted that under every circumstance 2+2=4! You just can't get any more dogmatic than that. But I have thanked God for her since then because I now do business with a bank that is equally narrow-minded. Also, when I figure my income tax I have found that the government has the same narrow-minded idea about 2+2. May I say to you, my beloved, truth is always dogmatic. And if it's not dogmatic, it's not truth.

Driving out of Portland, Oregon, one foggy day several years ago, we were going up to The Firs, a conference center in Washington, on a speaking assignment. Somehow I made a wrong turn and got off Highway 99. As I told my wife, "I don't understand how I got off with you and me both driving!" So I finally drove back into town because I was hopelessly lost. I drove into a filling station and asked the young attendant, "Can you tell me how to get to Highway 99?"

He thought for a moment. Then he said, "Let's see, I think you go that way—oh, no, I'm pretty sure it's down this street."

I asked him, "How long have you been here?"

"Two weeks."

"Thank you, but I'd better get better advice than that." I drove across the street and there was an older man in the filling station over there. I said to him, "Can you tell me how to get down to Highway 99?"

"I certainly can. You go down here two blocks. You come to a street light, you turn right, you go another block, and you are on Highway 99."

"Are you sure?"

He looked at me in amazement and said, "I'm *positive*."

He was a very dogmatic fellow, but I thanked God for him because he got me on Highway 99.

The Lord Jesus said, "I am the way, the truth, and the life; no man cometh unto the Father, but by me." And for almost two thousand years the Lord Jesus has been bringing men down the highway into His very presence. It's dogmatic, but it will bring you to the Father.

PHILIP

Then as our Lord moves out and on and up, another man interrupts Him—Philip, the quietest man among the apostles. You do not find him saying very much or doing very much, but every time you see him in action, he is bringing somebody to Jesus. Remember that Philip went and got a friend of his, a fellow who thought he was a humorist, who said, ". . . Can any good thing come out of Nazareth?" Philip didn't argue. He didn't talk much. He just said, "Come and see" (John 1:46). At another time the Greeks came to him, saying, "We want to see Jesus." Philip ran over to Andrew and asked, "What shall I do—some Greeks want to see Jesus?" And together they brought them to Him. We see Philip bringing folk to Jesus, but he didn't have much to say.

Here in the Upper Room Philip spoke out. He hadn't had much to say before, but I think he forgot himself. The other disciples were startled, I think, to hear Philip interrupting Jesus. But when a quiet fellow has something to say, it is usually worth listening to. And Philip voiced the basic longing of his heart:

> *Philip saith unto him, Lord, show us the Father, and it sufficeth us.* (John 14:8)

By the way, what is your ambition in life today? Is it to get rich? Is it to make a name for yourself? Is it even to do some wonderful thing for God? Listen to me, beloved. The highest desire that can possess any human heart is a longing to see God. Moses, who was so close to God, said, "If I could only see You" (Exodus 33:18–23). And here in the New Testament, Philip, in the Upper Room, says, "Show us the Father. That is all that I ask—just show us the Father." Would you today love to see the One who died for you? Personally, I would love to see the One who created this universe, who died for me, who has borne with me all these years. I would love to see Him. And someday we are going to see Him.

Philip's interruption did not sidetrack our Lord. Rather,

it occasioned one of His strongest statements concerning His deity.

> *Jesus saith unto him, Have I been such a long time with you, and yet hast thou not known me, Philip? He that hath seen me hath seen the Father; and how sayest thou then, Show us the Father?* (John 14:9)

The Lord Jesus says in substance, "When you look at Me, you look at God." Not 99.44 percent God, but you are looking at God in human flesh when you look at Jesus. This faces us with a dilemma: either He is God, the Savior of the world, or He is the greatest imposter the world has ever seen. There is no middle ground with Him. My friend, Jesus is God. Today He is the Savior of the world. And someday we shall see Him.

There in the Upper Room our Lord, after assuring these men that He was God and that He was returning to His Father, declared that they would be able to do greater works than He had done.

> *Verily, verily, I say unto you, He that believeth on me, the works that I do shall he do also; and greater works than these shall he do, because I go unto my Father.* (John 14:12)

"Greater works" are preaching the gospel from frail human lips and seeing the Spirit of God speak to human hearts so that men and women turn to God. For almost two thousand years it has been by the foolishness of preaching that multitudes of the human family have come to Christ. My friend, no *man* is equal to the task. Only a Savior who is at God's right hand has enabled us to do the "greater works" —because He has returned to the Father and the Holy Spirit has come into the world.

JUDAS

As our Lord continued, He was interrupted by another disciple who had an urgent question:

Judas saith unto him, not Iscariot, Lord, how is it that thou wilt manifest thyself unto us, and not unto the world? (John 14:22)

Sitting there was a man who was the first missionary, a man who had the first vision of a lost world, a man who really had a burden for other folk. The other men were so absorbed with other events that were taking place that they hadn't thought of the world outside. But Judas (notice that it is not Judas Iscariot, but the other disciple by that name), sitting there, says in effect, "Wait a minute, Lord. Aren't You forgetting something? You have brought us here to the Upper Room and You are telling us these wonderful things, but what about the world outside? Have You forgotten the world?"

Jesus answered, and said unto him, If a man love me, he will keep my words; and my Father will love him, and we will come unto him, and make our abode with him. He that loveth me not keepeth not my sayings; and the word which ye hear is not mine, but the Father's, who sent me. These things have I spoken unto you, being present with you. But the Comforter, who is the Holy Spirit, whom the Father will send in my name, he shall teach you all things, and bring all things to your remembrance, whatever I have said unto you. (John 14:23–26)

In other words, our Lord said, "No, Judas, I haven't forgotten the world. I am going back to My Father, and We will come to make Our abode with you. The Holy Spirit will teach you and bring to your mind what I have said so that *you* may go to the world with the gospel."

My friend, as we look out upon our disturbed world

today, although our Lord has not forgotten the world, it does look as though *we* have. He did not give us the tremendous truths of John 14 for ourselves alone. He has given us these things that we might pass them on to others.

In conclusion He said, ". . . Let not your heart be troubled, neither let it be afraid" (John 14:27). Today our Lord is at the right hand of the Father. And still today we frail human beings have questions. I've got a question. You've got a question. All God's chillun got questions. He is patient today. He is willing to deal with your problem, whatever it is. Maybe it's personal, personal failure like Simon Peter's. Maybe, like Thomas, you don't know the way of salvation. Maybe, like Philip, you have an overweening ambition and you haven't been able to reach your goal. Or, like Judas, you look out on the world and you wonder if God has forgotten it. Whatever your question is, bring it to Him. He has the answer today.

——8——

LIVING THE CHRISTIAN LIFE— GOD'S WAY

(Romans 8:1–23)

Before me is a letter, typical of many I have received recently, that tells the story of failure in the Christian life. The man writes,

> It seems that I know you because I have listened to you for so long. Several of your recent sermons have seemed especially for my encouragement, and, brother, do I need it. I am surely in the seventh of Romans, and cannot find the way out. I have the way, but cannot get in the eighth chapter. I am fighting a losing battle, seemingly single-handed.

The writer continues in this same frame of mind to the end of the letter which consumes several pages. It reveals a great distress and struggle going on within the heart of a man who apparently is a born-again Christian.

As we come to the eighth of Romans, we come to a chapter that is given to us to set before us the great deliverance that is ours. I have worked out a detailed division of it but will bypass that and just attempt to lift out its message as we go along. I trust there is something here that might

help a discouraged Christian. The purpose of the gospel
of Jesus Christ is to lift off the shackles from the human
family so that all might come into the place of salvation, and also to give power to those who want to live for
God, as does the writer of this letter from which I have
quoted.

Chapter 8 of Romans is one of the great chapters of the
Bible. You could not select ten of the great chapters of the
Bible and exclude the eighth of Romans. It is possible that
you could leave out John 14, you might omit Romans 12,
you might even leave out Hebrews 11, but you could never
leave out Romans 8.

One of the great saints of the past wrote, "If Holy Scripture were a ring and the epistle to the Romans its precious
stone, chapter eight would be the sparkling point of the
jewel."

Another has called it the Mount Whitney of Scripture.
The eighth chapter of Romans is a lofty, wonderful chapter. It opens with "no condemnation," it closes with "no
separation," and in between "all things work together for
good to those who love God." Now, friend, you can't have
it any better than that. Can you? It cannot be any more
wonderful than that. A preacher friend, Dr. Coy Maret,
put it like this: "No condemnation, no frustration, and no
separation." So just about all that we need is in this eighth
chapter of Romans.

Now it opens like this:

*There is, therefore, now no condemnation to them who
are in Christ Jesus, who walk not after the flesh, but
after the Spirit.* (Romans 8:1)*

The clause "who walk not after the flesh, but after the
Spirit" does not appear here in our better manuscripts but
is explained and appears in verse 4. However, a declaration

---

* Scripture quotations are from *The New Scofield Reference Bible.*

of the great truth that Paul has given us up to this point is that "there is now no condemnation to them who are in Christ Jesus."

This, by the way, is the sum total of what Martin Luther discovered in the Word of God. It was this epistle to the Romans which he was reading and studying that brought him to the place where he saw that no religious ceremony, no church, no *thing* he could do could bring him to God. The story has been found now to be accurate that Martin Luther went all the way to Rome, climbed up the Sancta Scala, trying to *do* something to make himself acceptable to God. And at that time the tremendous words came to him: "The just shall live by faith," and that it's not by the good works which we have done, but it's by "his mercy he saved us, by the washing of regeneration, and renewing of the Holy Spirit" (Titus 3:5).

The declaration, therefore, that introduces Romans 8 is: "There is, therefore, now no condemnation to them who are in Christ Jesus."

Now *that* is what salvation is. Salvation means to be *in Christ*. It does not mean to join a church or to *do* something. It means to be in Christ. Theologians have been looking for two thousand years to find a word that would describe our salvation. They have come up with the words propitiation, repentance, substitution, atonement, redemption, and justification, but the interesting thing is that the Bible also has a very simple word, the little preposition *in*. What does it mean to be saved? It means to be *in* Christ. And that is what justification is.

Now let's look at the expression "justification by faith." What does it mean?

Well, first of all there is the negative aspect. It means that you and I were hell-doomed sinners. You say, "Now look here, preacher, don't you talk to me like that!" Oh, no, friend, *I'm* not talking to you like that—*God* is talking to you like that. He says,

For all have sinned, and come short of the glory of God.
(Romans 3:23)

You say, "Now don't you try to tell me that I'm as bad as some of those bums down on skid row—thieves, winos and murderers." No, you are not. They are sinners. We will all agree to that when it's the other fellow, won't we? But you also have come short of the glory of God—maybe not as much as those fellows, but you have come short of the glory of God.

Let me give you an illustration. Suppose that today you would come to me and say, "Let's you and I play a game. Let's see which one of us can jump from downtown Los Angeles to the San Fernando Valley." Since I like jumping games, I agree to play. You say, "Well, McGee, I don't think you would be able to jump very far. Let's get others in the game." So a lot of people get in the game. It's a good game to play, by the way. Now I'd run and jump. I'll be honest with you, I don't think I would jump as far as I used to jump. Then you would come along and you would jump, and you would say, "Look, I jumped farther than you did." That probably would be true. All of us would jump, but we would all come short of the San Fernando Valley. No one can jump that far.

Now you may be better than somebody else, but regardless of who you are, you have come short of the glory of God. You have nothing that is acceptable to God. You stand before God as a sinner. Every person stands before Him as a sinner, a lost sinner. Therefore, when you and I come to God, we don't come offering Him anything. It is not by works of righteousness. We come to Him empty-handed, as lost sinners, and we trust Christ as our Savior.

Now there is also the positive aspect of justification. God not only subtracts our sin, He not only paid the penalty for our sin, but He does something else—He puts us *in Christ,* and God looks at us in Christ. My friend, you are completely saved in Christ or completely lost out of Christ. You are in Him 100 percent or out of Him 100 percent today. If you are in Christ, God sees you in Him, and you are as much accepted by God as Christ is! In fact, you have as much right in heaven as Christ has—or you have no right there at all because you and I have no right in and of ourselves. But in Christ we are accepted. As Paul wrote to the Ephesian believers, we are "accepted in the Beloved" (Ephesians 1:6). Now friend, you can't get any more saved than that. The poor lost sinner, the moment he trusts Christ is as much saved as he will be a million years from today.

Earlier chapters in the epistle to the Romans have covered this tremendous truth. Now the eighth chapter just reaches back and encompasses what has been said before, "There is, therefore, now *no condemnation* to them who are in Christ Jesus."

You see, there is no judgment for sin to those who are in Christ. If you are in Him, God sees you in Christ, and He accepts you because of Christ. Christ's righteousness is your righteousness. Certainly you and I have none of our own.

This is the great truth that gripped Martin Luther—the tremendous truth of justification by faith. And it shook the shackles off a darkened Europe. The Dark Ages rolled back like a flood, and the light of the glorious gospel of Jesus Christ broke over Europe. How to be righteous in God's sight has worried many men down through the ages. When Paul, you remember, came to Christ, he made this discovery. And to the Philippians he wrote:

And be found in him, not having mine own righteousness, which is of the law, but that which is through the faith of Christ, the righteousness which is of God by faith. (Philippians 3:9)

This is the righteousness of God which comes to us by faith only. And, friend, this is the righteousness that is available to you and me now. If today you have Christ and you are in Christ, there is no condemnation.

Paul is talking from experience because he is the man who fell on his face as a Christian. In Romans 7 he tells of this experience. He made such a blunder of everything and failed miserably. Now he goes on to talk about that:

> *For the law of the Spirit of life in Christ Jesus hath made me free from the law of sin and death.* (Romans 8:2)

Here he mentions the Spirit for the first time. We know that back in Romans 5 he mentions eight wonderful results of our justification by faith, one of which is that we *have* the Holy Spirit, but he doesn't mention the *work* of the Holy Spirit in the believer until he gets to the eighth of Romans. Now the reason he mentions it here is that this is the way of Christian living. You see, there is something that Paul discovered in the seventh of Romans, and it is this: Even after he was converted, he could not live the Christian life in his own strength.

A great many of us find this out the hard way. I remember that was my feeling. I thought when I got converted that I'd be walking on top of the world, but that is when I fell flat on my face. Never did I fall so flat as I did after conversion. Nobody had told me that I couldn't live the Christian life. In fact, they patted me on the back and told me I could. But I could not, and I found that out.

The Christian life is the Holy Spirit working through the believer, producing the life of Christ and what *He* wants. And anything that the Holy Spirit does not produce is of the flesh. It is no good at all, and it is not Christian living. Christian living is the work of the Holy Spirit.

There is no good in the old nature. Paul found that out. He said, "For I know that in me (that is, in my flesh) dwelleth no good thing . . ." (Romans 7:18).

Also he found that there was no power in the new nature. In verse 24 he cried out in dispair, "Oh, wretched man that I am! Who shall deliver me from the body of this death?" In other words, "I find that I can't do the things that I want to do. I'm a newborn Christian, and I want to live for God, but I can't do it!" Well, that is exactly what God said. He said you couldn't. Paul found it to be true, and I think everybody else has found it to be true. Just recognize it and realize it instead of trying to set your own goal. The man from whose letter I quoted at the beginning of this message has set a goal for himself, something he wants to do. He wants to be a businessman and dedicate everything he has to God. I judge from what he writes that he wants to be another LeTourneau. He asks, "God blessed Mr. LeTourneau. Why doesn't He bless me?" Well, maybe God doesn't want him to be another LeTourneau. Maybe He wants him to do something else. I do know this: The best way is not what you want and what I want; it is what the Spirit wants and what Jesus Christ wants in our lives. That is the Christian life—not some goal that you and I might set for ourselves.

Now the apostle Paul explains:

> *For what the law could not do, in that it was weak through the flesh, God sending his own Son, in the likeness of sinful flesh and for sin, condemned sin in the flesh, that the righteousness of the law might be fulfilled in us, who walk not after the flesh, but after the Spirit.* (Romans 8:3–4)

Here the Spirit is mentioned again. In the first seven chapters of Romans the Holy Spirit has been mentioned only one time, but in the eighth chapter the Holy Spirit is mentioned nineteen times. Obviously he is putting great emphasis on the Holy Spirit. Notice that he says, "What the law could not do because of the weakness of the flesh. . . ." I want you to see a wonderful truth in this.

Let me illustrate it with a story Dr. W. L. Pettingill used to tell. It meant so much to me, and I hope it will be helpful to you. He told the story of a good housewife who got a roast ready one day and put it in the oven to bake. Then she got busy doing other things. Later the phone rang—it was one of her neighbors who had just heard the latest gossip, so she sat down to listen. It developed into a long conversation, and all of a sudden she smelled something burning. She said, "I'm sorry, but I'm going to have to hang up. I smell my roast burning. I'll call you back later." So she hung up the telephone, rushed into the kitchen, opened the oven, and there was the roast—overdone and burning. She rushed to get a fork, reached down with it, and attempted to lift up the roast to get it out of the oven, but it wouldn't come—the fork went right through the meat; it just wouldn't hold. As I said, she was a good housewife, so she went and got the spatula, put the spatula down under it and a spoon on top. Then she lifted up the roast. What the fork could not do in that it was weak through the flesh, the spatula was able to do. There was nothing wrong with the fork, but there was something wrong with the flesh—overcooked. It wouldn't hold. So she had to use another method.

Now look, just as there was nothing wrong with the fork, there is nothing wrong with the Mosaic Law. When we say that we are not under the Law, we don't mean that the Law isn't good. It *is* good. It's God's Law. But, you see, it cannot save you. It's like that fork. It reached down in me, and it came right through. I don't know about you, but it couldn't lift *me* up. Has it lifted you up? Well, may I say to you, what the fork (the Law) could not do, God has sent His Holy Spirit to do. And the Holy Spirit in you can lift you up and enable you to live for God. That is the thing God is saying in this verse. The law could not do it because of the weakness of the flesh; now there is a new method, a new process, and that is by the Holy Spirit.

For they that are after the flesh do mind the things of the flesh; but they that are after the Spirit, the things of the Spirit. (Romans 8:5)

That word *mind* means "to obey," and that is the way it is used in my Southland. I remember holding meetings in middle Tennessee and being invited to a chicken dinner up in a country home one day. Oh, it was good chicken! The wife and mother fixed it and went out on the back porch to call her boy Willie. I tell you, that woman would have made a good hog-caller. Maybe she did call them, I don't know, but that day she was calling Willie. He never did answer her, and if he was a mile away he could have heard her. Finally she came in and said, "That young'un won't mind me anymore." Well, I knew what she meant, as did everybody else who was there. Paul uses this same word, "They that are after the flesh do mind the things of the flesh [that is, they obey the things of the flesh]; but they that are after the Spirit, [mind, obey] the things of the Spirit."

For to be carnally minded is death, but to be spiritually minded is life and peace. Because the carnal mind is enmity against God; for it is not subject to the law of God, neither, indeed, can be. (Romans 8:6–7)

The carnal mind is enmity against God. That is, man in his natural state is an *enemy* toward God. That old nature that we were born with is in rebellion against God. I wonder if you have ever felt this. Possibly at this moment you are enjoying the comfort of your home, but God wanted you to perform some service for Him. That is the weakness of the flesh, is it not? You could have gone if you'd wanted to go. The flesh, you see, didn't want to go. Now I have that kind of nature, you have that kind of nature—every child of God has that old nature. But if you live by that nature, everything you produce is just dead works. It won't amount to anything as far as God is concerned. You can't live for God if your motivation comes from the old nature. The carnal mind that you and I have is enmity against God.

Have you discovered this? Years ago a song was written with these words, "Prone to wander, Lord, I feel it, prone to leave the God I love." Is this your experience? Have you ever felt that? Well, somebody came along and said, "I don't think that is the experience of a child of God. I want to change it." And the words were changed to "Prone to *worship*, Lord, I feel it, prone to *serve* the God I love." Is that your experience? Well, which is correct? The fact of the matter is, friend, both of them are correct. Every child of God, if he is honest, would say, "Prone to wander, Lord, I feel it." Then there also are the times (thank God for those times) when we are living by the Spirit of God and can say, "Prone to worship, Lord, I feel it, prone to serve the God I love." You see, you have two natures. To be carnally minded is death, because the carnal mind is an enemy against God. To be spiritually minded—that's life and it's peace.

Also the interesting thing is that the carnal mind is not subject to the Law of God, nor can it be. Not only is our old nature an enemy against God, but it always will be that; it *cannot* be subject to the Law of God. And it never will be. God never has had an arrangement to save the old nature. God does not intend to save the old nature at all.

Now do not misunderstand me about this old nature that we have. All of us have it, we were born with it, and you would be surprised how limited that old nature is. I do not know about you, but when I was born into this world, I was born ignorant. I didn't even know *a* from *b*, nor did I know anything about manners at all. You talk about being born in darkness, we certainly are. I read recently a quotation from one of the latest scientific books in which it was pointed out that man is the only creature born into this world helpless, and that he doesn't know how to do anything except one thing—weep. That is all he can do without being taught! He has to be taught everything else. That's the old nature.

We come into this world very handicapped, don't we? We have to do something with that old nature as far as education is concerned. And I believe in education; I think we ought to get all of it that we possibly can. That old nature should be educated. Also it should be taught manners. I know they are going out of style, but they are something that we ought to have today. You need to teach little Willie to take off his cap when he comes into the house. You need to teach him to say, "Thank you," and "No, I don't care for the second piece of cake"—even then, chances are, he'll ask for it. But children need to be taught to be gracious, to be considerate of others, and to be respectful. All of those things have been taught to us. I remember as a boy how my mother used to try to instill manners into me. Oh, I thought I never would learn to be polite. It is something we've got to learn; we are not born that way.

This old nature that we were born with is against God. It will blaspheme, turn its back on God, deny Him in a minute. I've got a nature right now that, if it were not for His marvelous grace, would deny Him within the next five minutes. But, don't worry, I've found God's grace sufficient. Yet I have that old nature, and you have an old nature. We'd better reckon on it. We'd better realize that we have it.

Now God has no arrangement to salvage the old nature. God says it will finally die, but we won't lose it till we die physically. God has no program to restore old natures.

This is the reason He has given us a new nature, one that can become obedient to God. One characteristic of the new nature is that it *can* be obedient to God—but it needs empowering—it needs the Holy Spirit. So Paul says here:

So, then, they that are in the flesh cannot please God.
(Romans 8:8)

I do not know how much good you do—that is, what your neighbors call good—but regardless of what it is, if it is not of the Spirit it cannot be pleasing to God. You may be called upon by the Chamber of Commerce of your town tomorrow and be given a silver loving cup. They may say you are the outstanding citizen of your community, that you are philanthropic, that you are a good neighbor and you exemplify everything your community stands for. They may even go so far as to say that since you are a church member you are their idea of a Christian. But, my friend, if what you are producing in your life is just the works of the flesh rather than the fruit of the Spirit, none of that is pleasing to God. You see, it has to be of the Spirit of God working in your life. Therefore, you and I cannot boast of anything that we do because if there is any good, it is of the Spirit of God, it is not of us. If *we* do it, brother, it's not lovely at all.

> *But ye are not in the flesh but in the Spirit, if so be that the Spirit of God dwell in you. Now if any man have not the Spirit of Christ, he is none of his.* (Romans 8:9)

It may be that a Christian might say, "I don't have the Holy Spirit." My friend, if you have trusted Christ as your Savior, you *have* the Holy Spirit. "But," he may say, "I don't feel like it." Well, you don't know that you have Him by the way you *feel*. You have Him because God's Word says you do. In the fifth chapter of Romans it says that when you are justified by faith, the Holy Spirit is given to you and you are indwelt by the Spirit of God. That is the mark of a child of God.

> *And if Christ be in you, the body is dead because of sin, but the Spirit is life because of righteousness.* (Romans 8:10)

Notice that it says the body is dead because of sin. Somebody will ask, "When did it die?" Well, that was about two thousand years ago when *Christ* died for sin.

> *But if the Spirit of him that raised up Jesus from the dead dwell in you, he that raised up Christ from the*

dead shall also give life to your mortal bodies by his Spirit that dwelleth in you. (Romans 8:11)

The moment you trust Christ as your Savior, the Holy Spirit is given to you. The Spirit of God, the third person of the Godhead, comes to dwell in your heart and life.

Someone will say, "I'm not worthy of that." No, we certainly are not. God used three chapters in the epistle to the Romans to tell all of us that we are not worthy of it. He doesn't give the Holy Spirit because we are worthy; He does it because of His grace. He doesn't go into a community and say, "I'm looking for the outstanding people here that I might indwell them." Not at all. It seems to me as if He does the opposite, that He looks for the worst, the lost sinner who knows he is a sinner and will trust Christ. When one does that, the Spirit of God dwells in that person's heart and life.

Now we are told in verses 12 and 13:

Therefore, brethren, we are debtors, not to the flesh, to live after the flesh. For if ye live after the flesh, ye shall die. . . .

The natural man says he owes it to his flesh to satisfy it. He may rationalize his dishonesty by saying, "A man has to eat." A woman will say, "I live for sex, and I have to have my needs met." We hear this today on every hand. Satisfying the old nature has plunged our nation into the grossest immorality! But God says that we as believers are not debtors to the flesh. My friend, the flesh—and we all have it—is a low-down, dirty rascal. And we don't owe it anything.

. . . *But if ye, through the Spirit, do mortify the deeds of the body, ye shall live.*

You shall live as *sons.*

He is not talking here about salvation; he is talking about

Christian living. And we'll live as sons of God if we are walking in the Spirit, you see, and if we are putting to death the doings of the body. I get so tired of these people who are always talking about having crucified the flesh. I ask you, can you crucify it? Every time I do, it gets up and lives again. I've tried to beat it to death, but that doesn't do any good. My friend, that is not the way it is to be done at all. It is the deeds or doings of the body that we are to put to death. That is, we are to condemn and deal with those things in our hearts and lives that are wrong.

Now notice this wonderful statement:

> *For as many as are led by the Spirit of God, they are the sons of God.* (Romans 8:14)

If you are led by the Spirit of God, you are a son of God. The Lord Jesus gave the same picture when He said, "My sheep hear my voice, and I know them, and they follow me" (John 10:27). You see, He leads His own. The picture is of an Oriental shepherd and his flock of sheep. Perhaps a half dozen shepherds leave their flocks for the night in one fold. In the morning their sheep are all mixed up. One shepherd goes up over the hill there and calls his sheep. All of the sheep that know him come out of the fold and follow him. And this verse, "For as many as are led by the Spirit of God, they are the sons of God," speaks of the same thing. May I say to you, friend, that is the real test. Are you led by the Spirit of God? I appreciate the letter which I mentioned at the beginning of this message because I know it comes from a real born-again fellow. Although he is a sheep that has wandered away, he knows his Shepherd— that is, he is not following the wrong shepherd. "As many as are led by the Spirit of God, they are the sons of God."

> *For ye have not received the spirit of bondage again to fear; but ye have received the Spirit of adoption, whereby we cry, Abba, Father.* (Romans 8:15)

That word *Abba* was carried over from the Aramaic rather than being translated, and I'm glad the translators handled it that way. I have heard preachers say that the scholars did not know how to translate it. Of course they knew how to translate it. If you look it up, you will find it is an Aramaic word, and those who are acquainted with Aramaic will tell you what it means. However, it was such an intimate word, such a personal word, they felt that they would be irreverent, almost blasphemous, if they translated it literally. You see, the Holy Spirit within us cries up to the Father, and the word He uses is *Abba,* simply meaning "my daddy." It is an intimate word.

My friend, may I say to you that the Spirit of God cries out from the heart of a believer to God the Father, especially in times of trouble. When you are going through a struggle, when it looks dark for you, when you've been misunderstood, or when your friends have turned on you, it is at those times when the Spirit of God will bear witness with your spirit that you are a son of God, and the Spirit just cries out, "Abba, Father."

Thinking again of Martin Luther—my, how that fellow stood up against the hierarchy of his day! He is the man who said, "One with God is a majority." How could he stand against so many? Well, the Spirit was bearing witness with his spirit that he was a son of God. In that dark hour, Martin Luther tells us that he just cried out to God.

Have you had that experience? A very fine Christian, an outstanding man, was telling me the other day about a struggle that he went through. I said to him, "I don't see how you were able to go through it." And he said, "You know, McGee, when it looked like everything had fallen in upon me, when it seemed that everything had turned out wrong, my spirit just seemed to cry out to God in that dark hour. God has never seemed so close to me as He was at that moment." That is the mark of a real child of God. "For you have not received the spirit of bondage again to

fear; but you have received the Spirit of adoption, whereby
we cry, Abba, Father." How wonderful it is!

Perhaps you haven't had a trying experience, but sometimes God lets us have these trials so that we'll turn from
placing our confidence in man. We'll just look up to our
Father and cry out to Him, "Oh, my Father, my intimate,
personal Father!" And He is interested—He sees you,
knows you, and understands.

Then we are told:

> *And if children, then heirs—heirs of God, and joint
> heirs with Christ—if so be that we suffer with him, that
> we may be also glorified together.* (Romans 8:17).

Somebody is apt to get some wrong ideas at this juncture.
They may say, "My, if we are children of God like this,
indwelt by the Spirit of God, we can do anything we want
to do." No, you can't, friend. You are still in a frail human
body. Many of us have bodies that are limited and handicapped. Many of God's children are set aside for physical
reasons, and it's not God's will for them to be healed. Listen to this passage:

> *For I reckon that the sufferings of this present time are
> not worthy to be compared with the glory which shall
> be revealed in us.* (Romans 8:18)

One of these days you and I are going to get over yonder
and look back on this scene down here—on the struggle
that seemed so difficult, on the suffering that you went
through and I went through. I know there are a lot of folk
who have suffered in a way that I know nothing about.
Perhaps you have gone through the very fire. But when you
look back on it, friend, I think that you will say with me,
"Oh, that's nothing compared to what He had reserved for
me. I just wish I had suffered a little more, and I wish I

hadn't complained like I did." And we do complain down here, don't we?

For the earnest expectation of the creation waiteth for the manifestation of the sons of God. (Romans 8:19)

Why is it that we are suffering down here? Well, we are waiting, friend. God is working out a plan and program. He hasn't finished it yet, and that is the reason it's going as it is.

Not only did the curse of sin come upon man in Adam's disobedience, but the physical world came under the curse also.

For the creation was made subject to vanity, not willingly but by reason of him who hath subjected the same in hope. Because the creation itself also shall be delivered from the bondage of corruption into the glorious liberty of the children of God. For we know that the whole creation groaneth and travaileth in pain together until now. (Romans 8:20–22)

The creation is not delivered yet. All of it is travailing in pain until now. I call your attention to the fact that nature sings in a minor key. The wind blowing through the pine trees on a mountainside or the breaking of the surf on some lonely shore both emit the same sob. The frightened cry of some wounded animal pierces the night air. All about us is death and decay both in the animal and plant world.

Somebody said to me, "McGee, we've got healing in the atonement." I said, "Yes, I guess we do. We've got a new body in the atonement also, and there is going to be a new creation—but we don't have it yet, brother." We are waiting today, you see, waiting for that time.

And not only they, but ourselves also, who have the first fruits of the Spirit, even we ourselves groan within our-

selves, waiting for the adoption, that is, the redemption of our body. (Romans 8:23)

It hasn't come yet, but we are waiting for it.

When Christ comes, we are going to get rid of these feeble, infirm bodies that actually are a handicap to us. We are going to get new bodies. In the meantime we groan in these old bodies, waiting for the day when our redemption will be complete.

Between now and that glorious day, God has made every arrangement to keep those who are His own. Thank God, we have been indwelt by the Spirit of God, and we have been given a new nature. Now God wants us to live for Him.

When you and I go out on our own, asserting our own wills, trying in our own strength to live the Christian life—what happens? Why, we just fall right on our faces! We make a failure of it all. Even if you and I do produce something in the flesh which men may applaud, it is no good to God. It's of the flesh. Only that which the Holy Spirit produces in our lives can He accept. And that ought to be our prayer and our concern. Whatever we produce ought not to be the works of the flesh—not this backscratching, backslapping, parading kind of Christianity—but a deep, abiding faith in Jesus Christ which brings us to the place where we are dependent upon Him, where we look to Him and rest upon Him.

9

WALKING IN THE SPIRIT

(Galatians 5:16)

This I say then, Walk in the Spirit, and ye shall not fulfill the lust of the flesh. (Galatians 5:16)

In the staid, old-line denominations there has occurred a rash of the tongues movement. Why?

A Presbyterian pastor explained why he has gone into the movement: "What God had given them I wanted Him to give me! I still wanted to be a Presbyterian—and I hope to be one always—but I wanted to be a Presbyterian who was redeemed, filled with the Spirit, and walking close to God."

That's good. I like that. But—

I challenge you to drop in next Wednesday to the average denominational church and listen to the service that takes place there—*if* the church is open and has a midweek service. I do not think you will hear a Bible study. The man in the pew is ignorant of the Word of God because the man in the *pulpit* is ignorant of the Word of God.

There is a second explanation of why this has broken

out. It is the natural result of the first. In these denominations that have turned to liberalism, there is a hunger for something that is spiritual. The response to our radio programs throughout this country is helping us feel the pulse of people in our churches today. I am convinced that there is a great heart hunger on the part of many folk. They have been starved for so long that they are desperate in this hour. They have been fed for years on the barren husks of book reviews, philosophical pep talks, spineless theology, skeptical discourses, optimistic humanism, and Peale's psychology. One pastor announced his subject for the evening as "brief, bright, and brotherly." That is the type of message folk have been getting. Most denominational churches are like Mother Hubbard's cupboard—bare, with no spiritual food for their people. Many sincere people are hungry, and they do not know where to go for food in this hour. In their desperation, they turn to any direction and eat anything that is put before them, as a starving man would do.

While a careful study of the Bible reveals that God does not command us to speak in tongues, but rather lays down regulations to restrain the exercise of tongues (1 Corinthians 12–14), He *has* given to us clear-cut commands relative to our relationship with the Holy Spirit. These are of utmost importance! To obey these commands of Christ is to experience the power, the peace, and the joy which are God's will for all of His children today.

Some folk seem to think that they need to be all pepped up or hepped up—then *zoop*, up they go. But, my friend, you do not go into orbit living the Christian life; you walk on solid earth. The Christian life is not an occasional flight into space; it is a day-by-day walk—down the streets of our cities, in our neighborhoods, in our places of business, in our homes.

The believer is to walk in the Holy Spirit.

The Christian life requires a discipline that is far more demanding than that which is required by any ideology, any military service, or any organization. I suppose the reason for all the tragic failures, the frightful casualties, and the total wrecks that line the shore of life is that we have not taken seriously the command: *Walk in the Spirit.*

Walk in the Spirit literally means to walk by means of the Holy Spirit. It is in the present tense—*continue* to walk by means of the Holy Spirit. It is a constant, continual, habitual, unbroken walk by means of the Holy Spirit. It is a moment-by-moment walk. The walk of most of us Christians is up and down, off and on, hit and miss. But there should not be even a second when a child of God is not walking by means of the Holy Spirit.

By means of simply means that we are assigning to another that which we cannot do ourselves. Let me illustrate.

Suppose you boarded the train, the Super Chief, in Los Angeles, intending to go to Chicago. When the train reached the desert, it stopped. You waited and you waited and you waited. Wondering what was the matter, you got off, went to the rear of the train where you found the engineer trying to push the caboose! You would exclaim, "What in the world are you doing?" "I'm trying to get this train started." "But," you would say, "your place is up front. You just pull the throttle and the train will take off." You see, that diesel engine will do what a mere man cannot do.

It is ridiculous, I know, to imagine an engineer trying to push the Super Chief, but there are a lot of Christians today who are attempting to live just that way.

They are like the salesman in the south who came rushing into the station just as the train was pulling out. Thinking he still might make it, he took out at a run down the track with suitcase in hand. Every second the distance lengthened between him and the train. Finally he gave up and turned dejectedly back to the station. One of the natives, sitting on the lone express wagon, asked as he passed, "Did you miss your train?" "No," the salesman replied, "I just love to chase them out of the station." Christian living for a great many folk is just chasing the train out of the station. We never seem to get on board and leave to another what we cannot do ourselves.

God presents to us a new way of living. Paul expresses it as he writes to the Galatian believers:

> *For in Jesus Christ neither circumcision availeth anything, nor uncircumcision: but faith which worketh by love.* (Galatians 5:6)

It is no longer by law, no longer by works, but by faith (a new principle) working by love. It is a new formula, a new prescription, different from anything that has been offered in the past.

In the past, God said to His people,

> *And I will set my tabernacle among you: and my soul shall not abhor you. And I will walk among you, and will be your God, and ye shall be my people.* (Leviticus 26:11–12)

Back in the Old Testament God said to His people, "I will be *among* you. I will walk *with* you." But here is something altogether different. He says now, "I will walk *in* you." That is what it means to walk by means of the Holy Spirit.

We who have been saved by faith wonder why the unsaved rebel against the gospel of grace. Why do they feel they have to *do* something for God in order to be saved? God says they can do nothing but accept what He has done for them. He paid the penalty for sin by giving His Son to die. Christ died, He was buried, He paid the penalty in full, and He was raised in newness of life. Now faith in Him will save us! We marvel that the natural man rebels against accepting such a wonderful provision.

Yet how many Christians rebel against the walk of faith? That was the major problem with the Galatian Christians:

O foolish Galatians, who hath bewitched you, that ye should not obey the truth, before whose eyes Jesus Christ hath been evidently set forth, crucified among you? This only would I learn of you. Received ye the Spirit by the works of the law, or by the hearing of faith? Are ye so foolish? having begun in the Spirit, are ye now made perfect by the flesh? (Galatians 3:1–3)

Paul is saying, "You have been saved by faith, the Holy Spirit has regenerated you. Now you are to continue by the same method—walk by faith in the power of the Holy Spirit."

Christ is become of no effect unto you, whosoever of you are justified by the law; ye are fallen from grace. For we through the Spirit wait for the hope of righteousness by faith. (Galatians 5:4–5)

He is saying to them, "You were saved by *grace*—that is a high plane. Now do not drop down to a lower plane by attempting to live by law or some legal system. Continue to live by faith, walking in the power of the Holy Spirit."

If we can lay hold of this new truth, it will mean that a new day has dawned for us. It is a new life. We will experience a new joy, a new freedom, and a new peace. God wants us to live where there is the greatest fulfillment of life. He has the best for us, and He wants us to have His best, not His second best nor His third.

This great subject does not rest on a few isolated texts or on some "proof texts" and unrelated Scripture. It is the great theme of the Word of God. God wants His child to walk in the way that will bring the greatest amount of satisfaction and service.

Now there are three steps that must be taken in order to walk by means of the Spirit.

STEP ONE—REALIZE

In walking, you always have to take a first step. The first step in walking by the Spirit is a realization of our human weakness and sin. Because it seems like a strange beginning, many believers will not start there. But notice where God begins:

If we say that we have no sin, we deceive ourselves, and the truth is not in us. (1 John 1:8)

This is the most difficult step of all—always the first step is the most difficult. It is like the first step of a baby who stands there rocking, wondering whether he dare try that first step, afraid he might fall. He is moving out into something that is entirely new and he hesitates. For many believers this first step is new, and we are unwilling to take the place of utter helplessness and total corruption and absolute depravity before God. Many believers refuse this first step. "I am just as good as the next fellow. I don't do this and I don't do that." My beloved, self-satisfaction never leads you to a walk by means of the Spirit.

If we say that we have fellowship with him, and walk in darkness, we lie, and do not the truth: but if we walk in the light, as he is in the light, we have fellowship one with another, and the blood of Jesus Christ his Son cleanseth us from all sin. If we say that we have no sin, we deceive ourselves, and the truth is not in us. (1 John 1:6–8)

Actually we are not now talking about sins, but about the sin nature. When you and I came to Christ and trusted Him, we were given a new nature, yet that old nature abides with us. It is even more alert after conversion. That old nature which you and I have is a terrible thing, and frightful terms are used to describe it. John speaks of the *lust* of the flesh—that is the old nature. It is as a running sore filled with pus and corruption. Someone has said that if we could see ourselves as God sees us, we could not tolerate ourselves. Paul speaks of the old nature as a body of death, a putrifying corpse that we are carrying around. We cannot even embalm it, and it smells to high heaven! Now, don't you say that you do not have an old nature. Don't sit there and look pious as though all of this were far removed from where you live. My friend, every child of God has this old nature, and the greatest saints have been more conscious of it than anyone else.

David, with a broken heart, prayed, "Behold, I was shapen in iniquity, and in sin did my mother conceive me" (Psalm 51:5).

Isaiah, keenly conscious of his sin in the presence of God's holiness, cried, "Woe is me! for I am undone; because I am a man of unclean lips, and I dwell in the midst of a people of unclean lips: for mine eyes have seen the King, the LORD of hosts" (Isaiah 6:5).

Jeremiah, the weeping prophet, declared, "The heart is deceitful above all things, and desperately wicked: who can know it?" (Jeremiah 17:9).

Even the great apostle Paul had a sin nature, "O wretched man that I am! who shall deliver me from the body of this death?" (Romans 7:24).

Tholuck, the great German professor at Halle, at the banquet commemorating his fiftieth anniversary of professorship, when he was asked for what he was most thankful replied, "In review of God's manifold blessings, the thing I see most to thank Him for is the conviction of sin."

Count de Maistre of France was one of the great Protestant laymen. He said this, "I do not know what the heart of a villain may be, I only know that of a virtuous man, and that is frightful."

John Bunyan said, "When God showed me John Bunyan, as God saw John Bunyan, I no longer confessed I was a sinner; but I confessed that I was sin from the crown of my head to the soles of my feet. I was full of sin."

When the child of God comes to the place where he cries out in agony, "Who shall deliver me from this old nature that is dragging me down? I want to be free from the pull of a fallen nature," he has taken the first step toward walking by the Holy Spirit. Step one is a realization of our sin nature and our human weakness.

STEP TWO—RECOGNIZE

Now for the second step. There must be a recognition that God's standard for Christian living is not attainable by human effort or by human ability. Notice again these words,

> *Christ is become of no effect unto you, whosoever of you are justified by the law; ye are fallen from grace.* (Galatians 5:4)

The reason that we are not under the Mosaic law today—not under even part of it—is that God has called us to a higher plane of living. We are not to live on the low plane of the Law. God has set before us a standard that is infinitely higher and, humanly speaking, unattainable. God has already said that you and I *cannot* live the Christian life. It is impossible.

Now notice the standard God sets for His children today:

> . . . *Ye are a chosen generation, a royal priesthood, an holy nation, a peculiar people; that ye should show forth the praises of him who hath called you out of darkness into his marvellous light.* (1 Peter 2:9)

It is a standard of showing forth the praises of God! There are those who say that since we have been saved by grace, we can do as we please. Such is not the case. There are commandments for the Christian. No child of God can do as he pleases; he must do as *Christ* pleases.

The reason we are not under the Ten Commandments is that we have graduated to a higher level. Christ said:

> *A new commandment I give unto you, that ye love one another; as I have loved you, that ye also love one another.* (John 13:34)

Be honest now. Are you able to love another believer as Christ loves him? If you are truthful, you will have to say, "I fall short." God puts before us an impossible standard —yet these are Christ's commandments. He says:

> *If ye love me, keep my commandments. . . . If ye keep my commandments, ye shall abide in my love; even as I have kept my Father's commandments, and abide in his love. These things have I spoken unto you, that my joy might remain in you, and that your joy might be full. This is my commandment, That ye love one another, as I have loved you.* (John 14:15; 15:10–12)

This is a standard so high that we must fall down before God and confess that we cannot measure up to it in our own strength.

But this is not all. There are other commandments.

> *Furthermore then we beseech you, brethren, and exhort you by the Lord Jesus, that as ye have received of us how ye ought to walk and to please God, so ye would abound more and more. For ye know what commandments we gave you by the Lord Jesus.* (1 Thessalonians 4:1–2)

Then, turning to the last of this epistle, we find that he gives not ten commandments, but twenty-two! Here are a few:

> *Rejoice evermore.* (1 Thessalonians 5:16)

When you awake to a morning flooded with sunshine and the song of birds, and everything is coming your way, of course you rejoice! But what about that dark day, when your world has tumbled about you, when you were even betrayed by friends? Did you rejoice?

> *Pray without ceasing.* (1 Thessalonians 5:17)

We are to maintain an attitude of prayer, which means that our prayer does not end when we say "Amen." We are to move out in a workaday world in communion with God. Do you do that?

> *In every thing give thanks: for this is the will of God in Christ Jesus concerning you.* (1 Thessalonians 5:18)

How are you doing with that commandment? Do you give thanks for everything?

Paul, writing to the Corinthian Christians, said,

> *Casting down imaginations, and every high thing that exalteth itself against the knowledge of God, and bringing into captivity every thought to the obedience of Christ.* (2 Corinthians 10:5)

Is every thought that enters your mind brought to the obedience of Christ? When that fellow cut in ahead of you on the freeway this morning, was that thought brought to the obedience of Christ?

Oh, my friend, these are commandments that any honest person looks at and cries out, "I can't do it. I fall short!" God's standard is unattainable by human effort.

This realization is the second step in walking by means of the Holy Spirit. God wants us to know that we have this old nature that is in rebellion against Him—it never does anything right. When you take these two steps: (1) realizing your human weakness and sin, and (2) recognizing that

God's standard is unattainable by your own effort, then God is ready to meet you. This brings us to the third step.

STEP THREE—REST

The third and last step is to *rest* on the Holy Spirit—depend on Him to do for us that which we cannot do. This brings us back to our text.

This I say then, Walk in the Spirit, and ye shall not fulfill the lust of the flesh. (Galatians 5:16)

Now consider with me this matter of walking. We walk without thinking. We can go down the street thinking about something else while we are walking. But, you know, we had a great problem getting started. You may have forgotten, but notice that little fellow trying to take his first wobbly step and toppling over. Walking is something that if stopped for one second is not walking; it is standing. You have to keep going. You put one foot in front, then you have to bring up the other foot, and then you have to do it all over again. It is a moment by moment, a continual, a habitual thing.

It is interesting how the Word of God has brought together metaphors. The Christian life is a conflict, and in the conflict we are told to *stand*—"Stand therefore," Paul said to the Ephesians. Also, the Christian life is a race, and we are told to "*run* the race." But the greater part of the Christian life is just plain living, and that means *walking*—which is the most difficult. Many of us can move out onto the arena of life and when there comes the applause from the gallery we can draw our sword and stand our ground. Or when those on the sidelines are urging us to run, we can exert great effort. But when we get up in the morning to a sink full of dirty dishes or go down to the office to a desk loaded with accumulated work, we fail. It is then that we are to *walk* by the power of the Holy Spirit.

And we are to walk by faith and not by sight. Let us come back to Galatians 5:5, "For we through the Spirit wait for the hope of righteousness by faith." The whole Christian life, from the moment we are born again until we come into His presence, is a walk by faith—a faith that rests upon the indwelling Holy Spirit.

Let me use a homely illustration. I used to see a little old lady who moved about with the aid of a walker, a little enclosure on wheels. Here she would come down the sidewalk, only a short distance at a time, then she would stop and rest. As I used to watch her, I would think of the Christian life being something like that. And I long to get to the place to which she had come. My problem is that I say, "Oh, have done with this little cage I'm in. I'm strong enough to walk by myself." I do not take one step until I am on my face. Has that been your experience? We imagine we have the power and strength in and of ourselves to walk. We do not. We have to walk by the Holy Spirit. We must be utterly dependent upon and constantly resting upon the Holy Spirit, somewhat as that little old lady depended upon her walker.

My friend, you and I live in a difficult day. The devil is out to deceive us and to sidetrack us. We need to stay close to the Word of God. The entire bent of our lives should be to know Christ and to please Him. He reveals Himself and He reveals His will for us through His Word. Study the Word. See what He cautions against and what He commands. Appropriate the provisions He has made for our walk down here.

We need to start each day with God, *realizing* our human weakness and the presence of our old nature, *recognizing* and confessing to Him our inability to meet His standard, *resting* by faith in the power of the indwelling Holy Spirit to accomplish what we cannot do.

Beloved, if we live in the Spirit, let us also walk in the Spirit—for Jesus' sake.

── 10 ──

CHARGE IT

(The Epistle to Philemon)

The credit card has become the symbol of American business. It is the fraternity pin of the average American. It is the passport to plenty for a great many today. Anything can be bought with a credit card, from a gallon of gas to a ten gallon hat, from a sandwich to a chain of motels, from a night's lodging to a subdivision in Southern California.

There is a restaurant in Texas that displays insignias of all the different credit card organizations with the caption: *We Accept All These* and down underneath they add *We Take Cash Also*. When a purchase is made in any department store in the United States today, the classic cliche of the salesperson is "charge or cash?" and there's a slight look of disappointment if it's cash. You're immediately under suspicion when you're carrying that stuff around.

It may come to you as a bit of a shock to learn that Paul the apostle had a credit card even in his day—so they're not so new after all. In his letter to Philemon, we read:

If he hath wronged thee, or oweth thee anything, put that on mine account [just use my credit card, if you don't mind]. *I, Paul, have written it with mine own hand, I will repay it; albeit I do not say to thee how thou owest unto me even thine own self besides.* (Philemon 18–19)

So Paul the apostle could write to Philemon and say in effect, "Put it on my account, I'm signing now to put it on my credit card so you will know that I intend to pay this."

Behind that statement, of course, is a story. Back of the little missal of Philemon is a missionary. Back of this epistle is the apostle. Back of his promise is a person who will pay. Back of the charge is collateral, and back of the communication is a confidence that brings comfort to the heart.

I want us to see the background of this little epistle, for it tells its own story. Paul went to Ephesus on his third missionary journey. He spent two whole years there, and we are told in Acts 19:9,10 that the gospel sounded out from the school of Tyrannus during that period and by that method. It was a sounding board or, in a sense, a broadcasting station so that all who lived in that entire area "heard the word of the Lord." As a result, seven churches of Asia Minor came into existence. These are the seven churches to which our Lord directed the letters that we read in the first part of the book of Revelation.

Also there were other churches credited to Paul that he had never visited. People had come to Ephesus where he was preaching, heard the gospel, were converted, went back to their communities, and organized another local church. Such was the church of Colosse. Paul never visited it, as far as we know, although he is the founder of that church.

Now in the church of Colosse there was a very prominent man who was also a very rich man. His name was Philemon. Paul had led him to the Lord: "I Paul have written it with mine own hand, I will repay it; albeit I do not say to thee how thou owest unto me even thine own self besides" (Philemon 19). Now when this man was led to the Lord by Paul; as it generally happens when you are the

---

* All Scripture is from the *New Scofield Reference Edition*, unless otherwise noted.

instrument of leading someone to the Lord, Philemon felt indebted to him. Folk like that are generally the ones who are the most generous, by the way, and I think that was true of Philemon. After he came to know Christ, he probably came privately to the apostle Paul and said, "Paul, if you ever have need of anything or if ever I can do anything for you, do not hesitate to call on me. You are the means of my new birth. You are God's instrument, and I am perfectly willing to do anything for you that is at all possible for me to do."

Now Paul in this epistle is calling upon Philemon to do something, and this is what it was. This man, Philemon, owned slaves, as practically every man of means in the Roman Empire did. Before Philemon was converted (I have reason to believe it took place before) one of his slaves ran away. It was very common in that day, especially if a slave had been mistreated, although many times that was not the case, and we have no reason to believe that this slave had been mistreated.

The name of this slave was Onesimus, and the very interesting thing is that his name means "profitable" which leads us to judge that he had been profitable to Philemon. Many slaves in that day were made custodians of the children of the owner and often custodians of all his estate. Many of them actually acted as a fiscal agent so they could sign for the owner. The truth of the matter is that some owners were unable to sign their own names, whereas their slaves were educated. So this man Onesimus or "Profitable" evidently had been very profitable, and as a result he must have been put in charge and had a great deal under his supervision. He was a trusted slave and, of course, this opened up an avenue for him to escape. He could take advantage of it by reaching into the till of his owner and taking out whatever he needed for travel in that day.

Saying all of this reveals the open sore of the Roman Empire, that cancerous growth that finally sapped the strength of this mighty empire and brought it toppling down to the ground. The historian Gibbon says that one half of the 120 millions of people who populated the Roman Empire (60 millions of those people) were slaves. The slave was certainly not considered very valuable. One family in Rome had a retinue of 20 thousand slaves. Slave owners in that day were incredibly brutal. They had no regard for the lives of those under them. The plight of the slaves in the Roman Empire was hopeless. There was no place for them to flee. To go beyond the boundaries of the Roman Empire was the most dangerous thing for them to attempt, for the minute they crossed over, they would be picked up. The only way that they could possibly effect a successful escape was to go to some great metropolis and drown themselves in the great sea of the multitudes and mobs that were there. This, of course, made Rome the type of city that had to entertain the population with circuses and give them free food because many of those people were actually escaped slaves. No one could put his finger on them. It would be difficult, indeed, to identify any one of them.

Now the slave, because of his hopeless condition and the way he was treated, became morally corrupt and, in turn, he corrupted the youth of Rome. You see, the slaves were responsible for the instruction of the youth of Rome. The gross immorality that came into the Roman Empire came by way of the slaves teaching it to their young charges. Juvenal, the Roman writer, tells of a woman in Rome who had a slave killed just to see him die. The Emperor Augustus once interfered with a citizen who was about to throw a slave into a pool of voracious lamprey eels. Although Augustus intervened, don't think that he loved slaves, because the same Augustus Caesar under whose reign the Lord Jesus was born had a slave executed for the crime of killing a pet pigeon and a favorite quail of his. The slave had accidentally killed them, and as a result he was crucified—even as the Lord Jesus was. These instances are mere samples of the sadism that swept over the Roman Empire.

Virgil, another Roman writer, says there were three classes of implements, of chattels, in the Roman Empire. You divide them like this, vocal, semi-vocal, and dumb. The vocal were slaves, semi-vocals were animals, and the dumb were plows, chariots, etc. that they had around the place. When a slave stole (and many of them did—most were thieves) and was caught, he would be branded on his forehead with the letters CH, the Latin *Ceva Hurm,* meaning "beware the thief," and I'm sure that would have applied to Onesimus. He would have carried that mark to his dying day. A runaway slave had no rights whatsoever before Roman justice. A master could take him and do with him what he pleased. Onesimus was a runaway slave. He belonged to Philemon.

Onesimus finally made it to Rome. He wasn't too far from the border, but he didn't try for it. He knew his only hope was to get into some great metropolis, and we have every reason to believe that he hopped from Ephesus, then probably to Corinth and from there to Rome. There he buried himself in that great metropolis with the great population around him, thinking he would never be discovered —and the chances are he never would have been discovered.

But I can imagine one day Onesimus walking down the street. I do not think he is as happy with the freedom he has as he thought he would be. He certainly now has difficulty finding food—before, his master fed him. He has difficulty now of getting a place to sleep. Before, his master had that responsibility. So he finds that there was a freedom in slavery, and there is also a slavery in freedom. This man probably is not as happy as he could be. He's looking for entertainment, for Rome at this time certainly majored in entertainment, which explains the great Colosseum and all the entertainment that went on there. It was the emperor's way of keeping the mob satisfied in order that they might not take to the streets and riot.

In that mob was Onesimus. Walking down the street he

saw a little group, a knot of people gathered around some man. He was curious. He elbowed his way into the crowd and had his first glimpse of Paul the apostle, chained to a Roman soldier. In fact, he was chained to a soldier who belonged to the Praetorian Guard, which meant Paul was a special prisoner. He had appealed to Rome, but now he had freedom until his trial came up—that is, the freedom that the end of a chain would give to him—for he was chained to the soldier in his own rented quarters.

Paul was doing what he always did. God said when He first called Paul that He intended for him to appear before kings, and this he was going to do, and he already had. God said that he was to take the gospel to the Gentiles, and he is—there he is preaching on the streets of Rome and the crowd is around him.

Onesimus works his way up into the crowd and he listens. He hears this man talking about a liberty that is in Christ, a liberty that any slave would want and the kind of liberty that he had not found by running away, always running. But this man who is chained to a soldier is *free,* and he's found out that if the Son makes you free you're free indeed regardless of where you are or who you are. And this man, Paul the apostle, is preaching about the crucifixion of Christ. He's preaching about His resurrection. He's telling men and women to believe on Him, and some do.

Onesimus lingers after the others leave. He says, "I'd like to talk with you." And Paul leads this man Onesimus to the Lord. Paul tells us this in verse 10: "I beseech thee for my son Onesimus, whom I have begotten in my bonds." While he's chained to that Roman soldier, Paul leads this runaway slave to the Lord.

One day Onesimus came to Paul and said, "I have to talk with you. I have something to tell you." When everyone had left, he said to Paul, "You don't know who I am but I'm a runaway slave."

Paul said, "Where are you from?"

"I've come from the city of Colosse."

"There are many believers in Colosse. Who is your master?"

"My master is Philemon."

"Well, I led him to the Lord in Ephesus several years ago, and he owes me everything."

"Well, what must I do?"

"You have robbed your master, you've run away from him, and under this system you'll have to return. As a Christian, you'll have to go back to him. But I know this man and I happen to know his heart now, and when you go back you're going back differently from when you left. You left as a runaway slave. He was not a Christian and you were not a Christian. But now you're both Christians and that changes it."

Paul said in this letter to Philemon, "For perhaps he therefore departed for a season. . . ." Isn't that a lovely way of expressing it? The fellow hadn't planned to leave for a season, he'd left for eternity—Onesimus never intended to go back. "For perhaps he therefore departed for a season, that thou shouldest receive him forever." Listen to this: "Not now as a slave* but above a slave, a brother beloved, specially to me but how much more unto thee, both in the flesh, and in the Lord?" In other words, Paul now says to this man Philemon, "When he was with you, you called him Onesimus. He was profitable, but he became unprofitable. Now that you do not have 'Profitable,' he *is* profitable, and he will be valuable to you when he comes back."

This is the picture before us, and it is the story behind the headline that is here.

Now Paul sent this letter with Onesimus back to Philemon. A quartet of men left Rome one evening. I don't think the Roman government recognized that they were

---

* Since the Greek *doulos* is the word for both servant and slave, in the text of Scripture Dr. McGee substituted the English word *slave* rather than *servant* for historical accuracy.

carrying probably the most valuable documents that ever left Rome: the epistles to the Ephesians, the Philippians, the Colossians, and this little epistle to Philemon which Onesimus had tucked somewhere into his garment. He is on the way back to his master.

Now the question arises, what about slavery? Well, Paul is not discussing here the right or the wrong of slavery. I'd like for you to see that fact. I do hasten to say that the gospel, the coming of the Word of God, finally broke the back of slavery in this world. My beloved, everywhere the Bible has gone it has eventually ended slavery. It may take folk who are in the darkness of sin a long time, but their bondage is finally broken. In places where the Word of God has been taken away from the people, they go back into slavery. May I say to you, this is the Book and the only Book that has ever broken the back of slavery. But Paul is not discussing here the moral issue at all.

During the Civil War the North used the little epistle to Philemon to show that slavery was wrong, and by the same token the South used it to show that slavery was all right. Who was correct? Neither one was correct because this little epistle doesn't even discuss the right or wrong of slavery. Paul is not discussing the moral issue.

Then the next question is why doesn't Paul discuss the moral issue? We're living in a day when people want to be pragmatic, and they say that we should grapple with these issues directly. I say no. Paul was preaching a *gospel* that alone could destroy the awful curse of slavery. If he stirred up a revolt, it would cause an awful slaughter of slaves in the Roman Empire, for that happened time and time again, and Roman history bears testimony to it. In Rome a few years after this there was an outbreak led by one of the very capable ex-slaves which resulted in the slaughter of thousands of individuals. Paul is preaching a gospel that will do two things: It will change men's hearts, and then it will have a subsidiary effect upon society so that where this gospel is preached (even though men will not accept it) it will cause certain institutions to disappear.

For example, the great revival of John and Charles Wesley—although John Wesley never preached against slavery, never preached very much against drunkenness, I tell you, his preaching and the revival that resulted made England sober and delivered England from the revolution that came to France. And it also *ended slavery.*

My beloved, may I say to you that men's hearts need to be changed in our day. You may by direct action force people to do certain things, but until their hearts are changed you would create a dangerous situation. We need today to have this gospel preached again in America as it was preached years ago during the days of Finney and the days of Moody. If it were preached, it would solve 90 percent of the problems that we have today in this nation. We're going at the problem from the wrong direction. Paul went at it from the right direction. He knew that the gospel would sooner or later break the back of slavery, for no longer can Philemon treat Onesimus as a slave. Paul says, "He's your brother," and when a man is your brother you won't make him your slave.

What a transformation has taken place in this picture and in the home of Philemon!

When I read the epistle to Philemon I feel that I'm reading a personal letter that was not intended for public gaze. I am confident that when Paul wrote this little epistle he did not recognize that the Spirit of God was going to include it in the Bible. Now, he did know it when he wrote Romans. He knew it when he wrote 1 Corinthians. He knew it when he wrote Ephesians. But when Paul wrote to Philemon he was just opening up his heart and being very personal.

The first year I was in college each freshmen was assigned to room with an upper classman, and I was put with one that I was glad to leave after the first semester. I found him one day reading my personal mail! And in order to get even, I began to read his mail. But I didn't do it very long.

The reason I quit was that I had such a guilty feeling reading somebody else's mail. Well, I have that same feeling when I read Philemon. I feel like it's a private letter and it always is a little embarrassing to read somebody else's mail. Here Paul opens up his heart in quite an unusual way.

He says, "I'm sending Onesimus back to you." Evidently Onesimus was a trained man. He may have had a real gift for handling sensitive matters. Paul is now in prison, tied to a Roman soldier. He can't navigate about, and there are many things he would like to have done. When Onesimus was saved, Paul thought, *My, it would be wonderful to have this fellow here with me to be my assistant, to run on errands and to do other things for me.* He thought along that line. The fact of the matter is that he was almost on the verge of doing it, but then he said, "No, I can't do that. It would not be honorable. I must send him back to his master."

Notice what he wrote: "Whom I have sent again; thou, therefore, receive him, that is, mine own heart" (Philemon 12). That's the way we would say it, but in the original the word is *bowels*, "mine own bowels." Now, don't be afraid of that expression. After all, TV is pretty plain today. What he's talking about here is that which is psychological. You know, they've found out now that there are actually two places where you and I live and move and have our being. One place is the head, and not much happens up there—you've probably discovered that! But honestly, we live and move and have our being down lower in the body, as Paul is saying here. In other words, "When you receive Onesimus, you're not receiving a runaway slave who deserves to be crucified or to have the 'thief' brand put on him. No, you are receiving the *heart* of the apostle Paul, and that's the way I want you to treat him."

Now listen to Paul, "Whom I would have retained with me, that in thy stead he might have ministered unto me in the bonds of the gospel" (Philemon 13). Believe me, Paul is really opening up, isn't he? In essence he says, "I thought about retaining him in your stead—because you said you'd do anything for me—that he might be helpful to me since I'm here in prison. But I thought it over and will do the Christian thing."

"But without thy mind would I do nothing, that thy benefit should not be, as it were, of necessity but willingly" (Philemon 14). If Paul had sent the letter back without Onesimus himself, Philemon might say, "Yes, that's all right, but Paul put me on the spot, and I have to do it because he forced me to do it." In effect Paul says, "I'm sending him to you, and if you want to send him back to me, that's all right."

I do not know this—we have no further word, but I think that on the return boat to Rome Onesimus was on board, coming back to minister to the apostle Paul.

Notice that Paul is talking about something quite wonderful in verse 16, "Not now as a slave, but above a slave, a brother beloved, specially to me but how much more unto thee, both in the flesh, and in the Lord?"

Back in verse 11 Paul played on the two words "Onesimus" and "not-Onesimus"—profitable and unprofitable. He says, "Who in time past was to thee unprofitable, but now profitable to thee and to me." It is interesting that when the man became a Christian he became profitable; he became valuable. He wasn't before. What a value is put upon a man when he becomes a child of God! What a different man it makes him, if you please. Now he says here, "Not now as a slave, but he's a brother to you now." The minute that a person comes to Jesus Christ and accepts Him as Savior, he's brought into the body of believers. And in that body of believers, according to Galatians 3:26 and 28, something wonderful takes place: "For ye are all the sons [children] of God by faith in Christ Jesus. . . . There is neither Jew nor Greek, there is neither bond nor free" [they are not now Philemon the owner and Onesimus the slave] "there is neither male nor female; for ye are all one in Christ Jesus."

A new relationship has been established between Philemon and Onesimus.

Actually this is the only real integration the Word of God knows about, and this is an integration which has nothing to do with color, nothing to do with race, nothing to do even with the sexes, but it has everything to do with a person coming to Christ. If a person has not come to the Lord Jesus Christ as his Savior, he is not a child of God. The most damnable heresy in the world today is the so-called universal fatherhood of God and universal brotherhood of man. The Bible knows nothing about it. Our Lord even said to the religious rulers, "Ye are of your father the devil . . ." (John 8:44). The one brotherhood that the Word of God knows about is that brotherhood that's in Christ today. When a Jew and a Gentile, a free man and a slave, a rich man and a poor man, male and female come to Christ, they are brought into a brotherhood where they are made one in Christ, my beloved. That is the brotherhood that the Word of God knows something about, and it is real. It absolutely revolutionized the home of Philemon. Note what Paul said about him in the first seven verses. It revolutionized his business relations. It revolutionized his relationship with people—even with this man Onesimus, a runaway slave who had stolen from him. Why?

Will you notice what he says now in verses 17 and 18: "If thou count me, therefore, a partner, receive him as myself." I think the conversation went something like this: Philemon, you always said to me, "Paul, I hope in your busy ministry you'll be able to come to Colosse someday. I have a beautiful, palatial home and a lovely guest room. When you come and visit me, I'm going to put you in that guest room." Paul says, "If I can ever find time I'll be glad to come over and visit you," but he never found time. Paul never did visit Colosse, but here he says, "Onesimus is coming. You're not going to crucify him. You're not going to beat him. You're not going to mistreat him. I want you to receive him just as you would receive me. Put him in that lovely guest room you have."

That's not all. Paul continues, "If he hath wronged thee [and he had], or oweth thee anything [and he surely did], put that on mine account." In other words, "Charge it. Here's my credit card. Onesimus can't pay. Charge it to me. I will repay it."

This scene now sinks into the shimmering shadows of the past. This incident that concerned the Apostle Paul and two believers in the early church now fades into the halls of history. I see another scene, a present-day scene, one that is being enacted right today, has been reenacted in my life, and if you're a child of God it has been reenacted in your life. I see the throne of God, and I see the Lord Jesus Christ sitting at His right hand, and I see a fellow who was a sinner by the name of Vernon McGee coming to God for forgiveness. The Word of God told me I was a slave of sin and that I was a runaway slave because I was in rebellion against God. I had wronged Him. I was a sinner. I was lost. A holy God could not receive me. The Son who had come down here about two thousand years ago and died on a cross turned to the Father and said, "If he hath wronged thee, or oweth thee anything, put that on My account—I paid his penalty when I died on the cross. I paid the price."

Years ago in my Southland a fine young black fellow made application to a church for membership, and the deacons were meeting to examine him. Believe me, they were fundamental, and they asked him the question, "How did you get saved?" This young man said, "Well, I did my part and God did His part." Knowing that salvation is the *gift* of God, not of works, the deacons asked him, "What was your part? And what was God's part?" He said, "My part was the sinnin'. God's part was the savin'. I done run from Him as fast as these rebellious legs and this sinful heart could carry me, and He done took out after me until He run me down."

My friend, that's the way I too got saved. That's the way you got saved, if you did. Jesus paid it all. He is the One who has the credit card today.

> *Jesus paid it all,*
> *All to Him I owe;*
> *Sin had left a crimson stain,*
> *He washed it white as snow.*

That's not all. "If thou count me, therefore, a partner, receive him as myself" (verse 17). Certainly the Lord Jesus is a partner with His Father. He is equal with the Father. The Father and the Son are one, and they have one mind. The Son says, "I want You to receive him just as You receive Me." My friend, and I'm being reverent when I say this: at this moment you have as much right in heaven as Jesus Christ has or you have no right there at all. You are either completely, perfectly saved in Him or you are completely lost apart from Him. The Son said to the Father, "I want You to receive Vernon McGee just like You receive Me," and that's the way He receives you, "accepted in the beloved." My friend, you can't be saved any more than you are today if you are in Christ. A million years from today you're going to find that I am much improved—I hope so! But I won't be any more saved a million years from today than I am right now because I am in Christ. The Bible says in Romans 8:1, "There is, therefore, now no condemnation to them who are in Christ Jesus. . . ." What a picture is in this practical little epistle! It worked itself out in the first century of the Roman Empire and revealed that Christianity was the reality. May I say that for about twenty centuries it has been working its way out in the lives of multitudes.

Paul is gone. Onesimus and Philemon have already played their parts and have disappeared from the scene. But you are here today, and God the Father and God the Son are yonder, and God is prepared to receive you. He *wants* to receive you. He loves you because the Lord Jesus came down here and paid the penalty for all your sins.

Don't argue with me that Onesimus was not worthy to occupy the guest room in the home of Philemon. He certainly was not, but somebody else was worthy, and somebody else made it possible for him because somebody loved him. I'm not worthy of heaven and you're not worthy of heaven, but Somebody loved us, and Somebody gives us His standing there!

Either your sin today is on you or it's on Christ. It can't be on a third person. You can't transfer it to anyone but Him. He's the only One who is willing to take your sin. He bore it. Christ said, "Put it on My account." He paid the penalty for it. He wants God to receive you, and God will receive you as a son! Will you receive Him?

— 11 —

WHY DO GOD'S CHILDREN SUFFER?

(Hebrews 12:3–15)

For consider him that endured such contradiction of sinners against himself, lest ye be wearied and faint in your minds. Ye have not yet resisted unto blood, striving against sin. And ye have forgotten the exhortation which speaketh unto you as unto sons, My son, despise not thou the chastening of the Lord, nor faint when thou art rebuked of him; for whom the Lord loveth he chasteneth, and scourgeth every son whom he receiveth. If ye endure chastening, God dealeth with you as with sons; for what son is he whom the father chasteneth not? But if ye be without chastisement, of which all are partakers, then are ye bastards, and not sons. Furthermore, we have had fathers of our flesh who corrected us, and we gave them reverence. Shall we not much rather be in subjection unto the Father of spirits, and live? For they verily for a few days chastened us after their own pleasure, but he for our profit, that we might be partakers of his holiness. Now no chastening for the present seemeth to be joyous, but grievous; nevertheless, afterward it yieldeth the peaceable fruit of righteousness unto them who are exercised by it. Wherefore, lift up the hands which hang down, and the feeble knees; and make straight paths for your feet, lest that which is lame be turned out of the way; but let it rather be healed. Follow peace with all men, and holiness,

155

without which no man shall see the Lord; looking dili-
gently lest any man fail of the grace of God, lest any root
of bitterness springing up trouble you, and by it many
be defiled.

—Hebrews 12:3–15*

Our subject is a perennial question which occurs constantly and monotonously more than any other Bible-re-
lated question. It is a question which is asked with a capital
WHY? by both believer and nonbeliever. There have been
more books written on this subject than the subject of the
Antichrist or the social gospel or how to live the Christian
life. And still the question is being asked, "Why *do* God's
children suffer?"

One of the factors which has added to the perplexity and
complexity of the problem is the unbiblical sales pitch to
the unsaved that is given in some quarters. It is claimed
that if you will only trust Christ you will move into the
green pastures where all is calm and the problems of life
are solved. Even prosperity and healing abound as a bonus
for believing. Another addition is joy without any sorrow
and with no cloud to darken the sky. In other words,
Christianity has been made an inoculation against disease
and trouble. One book that was sent to me recently showed
how you could make a million dollars by coming to Christ.
At least the author did it, and he said that anyone could do
it. The book didn't help me at all, I can tell you that! Such
promises are, to my judgment, totally unscriptural. They
sound, however, very good. They appeal to the natural
man. And they even sound scriptural.

Let's understand one thing: Salvation is a redemption
paid by Christ for the penalty of your sin and my sin. And

---

* Bible quotations in this chapter are from *The New Scofield Reference Bible*.

the primary benefit is that a hell-doomed sinner is now going to heaven because Jesus died in his stead, and the Holy Spirit has brought conviction of sin into his heart and life while he was still "dead in trespasses and in sins."

Now I don't want to be misunderstood. There is joy in the Christian life. There is peace. And there is healing. I know. I have experienced all three of these, and I can testify that all of them are certainly true.

However, it is an axiom of the Christian life that God's children suffer. There is no escape from it. Savonarola put it like this, "A Christian's life consists in doing good and suffering evil." That is the picture he paints, and down through the ages God's men have painted that kind of a picture. In fact, the Word of God is very clear in this connection. If you go back as far as Job, which would take you back probably to the time of Moses or even to Abraham, you will find that he illustrates this truth by a great law of physics:

> *Yet man is born unto trouble, as the sparks fly upward.*
> (Job 5:7)

According to the laws of aerodynamics, because of the heat being generated, sparks will fly upward. Just as that is true, man must experience troubles. We will face trouble in this world. David wrote:

> *Many are the afflictions of the righteous; but the LORD delivereth him out of them all.* (Psalm 34:19)

And actually the Lord Jesus told His own (sometimes I think we forget Scriptures like this):

> *These things I have spoken unto you, that in me ye might have peace. In the world ye shall have tribulation: but be of good cheer; I have overcome the world.*
> (John 16:33)

Paul likewise makes the dogmatic assertion:

> *Yea, and all that will live godly in Christ Jesus shall suffer persecution.* (2 Timothy 3:12)

There is no if, and, but, or perhaps about that at all. It is an axiom of Scripture that God's children suffer.

God's child is not promised that he will escape pain, disappointment, and sorrow in this life. Annie Johnson Flint has expressed it in a lovely way.

WHAT GOD HATH PROMISED

> *God hath not promised skies always blue,*
>   *Flower-strewn pathways all our lives through;*
> *God hath not promised sun without rain,*
>   *Joy without sorrow, peace without pain.*
>
> *God hath not promised we shall not know*
>   *Toil and temptation, trouble and woe;*
> *He hath not told us we shall not bear*
>   *Many a burden, many a care.*
>
> *God hath not promised smooth roads and wide,*
>   *Swift, easy travel, needing no guide;*
> *Never a mountain, rocky and steep,*
>   *Never a river, turbid and deep.*
>
> *But God hath promised strength for the day,*
>   *Rest for the laborer, light for the way,*
> *Grace for the trials, help from above,*
>   *Unfailing sympathy, undying love.*

You see, God did not promise we would miss the storms of life. He only promised that we would make the harbor at last.

Scripture makes abundantly clear, not only the fact that God's children do suffer, but the reasons God's children suffer. My friend, trials would be meaningless, suffering would be senseless, and testing would be irrational unless God had some good purpose and sound reason for them. Or, as it has been put, "God nothing does, nor suffers to be done, but what we would ourselves—could we but see through all events of things, as well as He."

There is no pat answer to the problem of why God's children suffer. It is not a simple question that can be answered with one verse of Scripture. People frequently ask me, "Can you give me a verse of Scripture for that?" Well, there are a great many truths in the Word of God that you don't have an isolated verse for, I can assure you.

After I had been laid aside for several weeks one summer with severe illnesses, I had an opportunity to study Hebrews, chapter 12. I had reached that chapter in making tapes for the *Thru the Bible Radio* program. My doctor wouldn't permit me to make tapes, but he allowed me to do what he called my paperwork. So I was able to continue studying and I spent a great deal of time in this twelfth chapter. I found that I was studying it, not from the position of a spectator-saint, but from the position of one who was then in the arena of suffering.

REASONS FOR SUFFERING

Now I want to suggest to you seven reasons that God's children suffer. You may discover others, but I do think these are comprehensive and cover the field fairly well. But first let me put down another axiom of Scripture: God can prevent His child from suffering. I don't think anyone would argue that point. The question is, of course, why doesn't He? Why has not God kept His children from suffering—especially the severe suffering that a great many saints have had to go through?

The First Reason—Stupidity

The first reason God's children suffer is for our own stupidity, our own willfulness, our own selfishness, and our willful ignorance. Many times we try to blame God for this kind of suffering, but it is our fault.

> *For what glory is it if, when ye are buffeted for your faults, ye shall take it patiently? But if, when ye do well and suffer for it, ye take it patiently, this is acceptable with God.* (1 Peter 2:20)

Now the word here for "faults" is the Greek word *hamartano,* which means to miss the mark. It is a picture of a man with a bow and arrow who is shooting at a target. He comes short of that target, which simply means he misses the mark. Many of us today because of our willfulness, because, actually, of our stupidity, miss the mark in many judgments that we make.

I could enlarge on this, but let me cite a couple of illustrations. Did you ever invest in a wildcat oil well in Texas? If you did, you were stupid! Anyone who would do a thing like that is stupid. Somebody says, "But I knew a man who invested and made a fortune." Yes, one out of perhaps a million has that happen to him, it's true, but what chance do you have of being that one? I know a young man who inherited quite a sum of money. He and his wife could have lived comfortably the rest of their lives on what he inherited. But he invested in oil wells and they were all dry holes. He lost a fortune. I have heard his wife say several times, "Why did God let this happen to us?" Well, I don't think God let it happen to them. I think they were stupid. They missed the mark in their judgments.

Also there are those who get out of the will of God. A man came in to see me, when I was a pastor in downtown Los Angeles, with a real problem. In fact, he had a wife who proved unfaithful to him. He was going to get a divorce. As I was expressing my sympathy to him for his very unfortunate state in life, he said, "It's my own fault." And he used the term *stupid.* He said, "I was stupid." He had come out to California during the war, was stationed out here. He said, "I was a Christian, and at that time I thought I wanted to do God's will, but before long I drifted out of the will of God. I got into sin and I met this girl who was unsaved. I married her, and I've lived in a hell ever since." Well, he understood. He didn't blame God for it. And many of us suffer because of our own stupidity.

The Second Reason—A Stand For Righteousness

The second reason God's children suffer is for taking a stand for truth and righteousness. Again I turn to 1 Peter:

> *But and if ye suffer for righteousness' sake, happy are ye; and be not afraid of their terror, neither be troubled, but sanctify the Lord God in your hearts, and be ready always to give an answer to every man that asketh you a reason of the hope that is in you, with meekness and fear.* (1 Peter 3:14–15)

In other words, Peter is saying here that when trouble comes to you because you have taken a stand for righteousness, first be sure you are right and that you have a right relationship with Jesus Christ. Then when you are sure of that, you can take your stand knowing that God will see you through. I know a man who was an official in a very large corporation—its headquarters were in Chicago and he was the western representative. They wanted to give him a promotion and make him one of the vice-presidents. But in that office he would have had to entertain customers by cocktail parties and procuring other forms of entertainment for them. So he refused it. He said, "I am a Christian. I won't do that." It cost him the promotion, and he was actually demoted. But he was willing to make that sacrifice. It cost him something to take a stand for righteousness. And I believe, friend, that any Christian who takes a stand for God today will somewhere along the line have to pay a price for it.

The Third Reason—Sin

There is a third reason God's children suffer. We suffer for sin in our lives. If a child of God commits sin, does he get by with it? The answer, of course, is no. But God says that He will give us an opportunity to judge sin in our lives.

For if we would judge ourselves, we should not be judged. (1 Corinthians 11:31)

In other words, when we sin God gives us an opportunity to confess that sin and make it right. If we do that, God will not judge us. But God says in effect, "You are My child and if you commit that sin, I'll take you to the wood-shed—if you won't deal with it yourself." And, friend, if He doesn't take you to the woodshed, you are not His child because He never whips the devil's children, only His own. If we don't judge ourselves, then God says, "I will judge you." And I think that is what John meant when he said there is a sin unto death (1 John 5:16), meaning physical death for a child of God. In other words, a child of God can go just so far, he can commit certain sins for which God will take him home, remove him from this life. A child of God cannot get by with sin.

There are two good Bible illustrations of God's dealing with the sins of His children. In the Old Testament it is David. Now David committed two awful sins. He broke two of the Ten Commandments. David is God's man. Will he get by with it? Well, he thought he had, and how long he concealed it we do not know. David, I think, came in, sat down on his throne, looked about him at his court, and thought, *I wonder if anyone knows.* He came to the conclusion that no one knew, so he went on with the state business. There was brought before him the different ones who represented other governments, those with complaints, and so forth, and one day there slipped into the group a man who actually was a very fine friend of David's. He was Nathan the prophet. I think David said, "Hello, Nathan," not thinking that he knew anything about his hidden sin. And when there was a lull in the business of the court, Nathan said, "I have a little story I'd like to tell you." You will find this incident recorded in 2 Samuel 12.

Nathan told him about two men in his kingdom. One was a very rich man with flocks and herds. The other was a poor man with just one little ewe lamb. He loved that little lamb and had raised it with his children. Then a visitor came to see the rich man and, instead of reaching into his own flock and taking a lamb for the visitor's dinner, the rich man went over and took the pet lamb that belonged to the poor man and killed it. David, who was redheaded, stood up in anger. (It is interesting how we can always see the fault in the other fellow. We can clearly see the other person's sin, but it is difficult to see our own!)

David said, "As the LORD liveth, the man who hath done this thing shall surely die!" I tell you, that's righteous indignation on the part of David.

But Nathan, who is the bravest man in the Bible in my opinion, pointed the finger and said, "Thou art the man."

Now David could very easily have denied that he was guilty. He could have just lifted his scepter, and his servants would have taken this man Nathan out and executed him. Nobody would have been the wiser. But that's not what David did. He bowed his head and confessed, "I have sinned." You see, David had tried to conceal his sin. Instead of confessing it to God after he had done it, he went on to commit a far greater sin, and was attempting to rationalize that. So God took him to the woodshed, and He never took the lash off his back. Very frankly, when I read the story of David, I feel like saying to the Lord, "You've whipped him enough!" But *David* never said that. He went through it without complaining because he wanted the joy of his salvation restored to him. He wanted to be back in fellowship with God. So David learned that God judges sin in the lives of His children.

Then in the New Testament, in Acts 5, Ananias and

Sapphira illustrate the sin unto death. I believe they were children of God. And they lied. In the early church they could not get by with a lie. Death isn't the immediate result today, by the way, but because the early church was a holy church, they couldn't get by with it. God judged them. They committed a sin unto death, and God took them home because God will deal with His own children.

The Fourth Reason—Past Sins

The fourth way in which God's children suffer is that we suffer for our past life of sin—committed even before we were saved. Now I want to be very careful here because a great many people will say, "But since I came to Christ, doesn't that mean all my sins are forgiven?" Yes. If you've accepted Christ, you will never come before Him for judgment which will affect your salvation. Never! "Well, if I committed a sin before I was saved, do you mean to tell me that I suffer for that?" You surely will. Listen to Paul as he writes to the Galatians:

> *Be not deceived, God is not mocked, for whatever a man soweth, that shall he also reap.* (Galatians 6:7)

What kind of a man is he referring to? A Christian man. Paul is writing to believers. We reap what we sow. This is, I think, applicable to people in any walk of life, whether they are believers or nonbelievers. But Paul is writing to believers, and he says we are going to reap what we sow.

That principle is at work everywhere in the physical world. You sow corn and you reap corn. You sow peanuts; you reap peanuts. You sow cotton and you reap cotton. You plant an orange tree, and you're going to pick oranges someday. "Whatever a man sows, that shall he also reap."

Saul of Tarsus, a brilliant young Pharisee who hated Jesus and hated Christians, stands one day while men bring their outer garments and put them at his feet. Then he gives the signal to begin the stoning of Stephen, which puts another young man to death. "But," you say, "Paul was converted on the Damascus Road. God has forgiven him." He certainly has. Paul is on the way to heaven. You can be sure of that. But, you see, he committed an awful sin. And so on his first missionary journey, while he is in Lystra one day, they drag him outside of the city and stone him and leave him for dead. (I believe he *was* dead, and God raised him from the dead.) You never hear Paul complain about the stoning. Paul knew that whatever you sow, you reap— he's the one who wrote these words to the Galatians.

Mel Trotter, who was one of the great evangelists in my generation, held meetings for us when I was a pastor in Nashville, Tennessee. After a service one night, a group of us went over to Candyland. Everyone else ordered a big malt or milkshake, but he ordered a little glass of water. That was all. Mel Trotter was a converted drunkard and probably had sunk as low as any man could sink. He even had stolen the shoes, which the neighbors had bought, off the feet of his little dead daughter when she was in her coffin—took them out and hawked them to buy liquor in order to get enough courage to go to the funeral. You just don't go any lower than that! Yet God had saved him, and he had become an outstanding evangelist. So as we were enjoying our malts we began to kid him because he had only a little glass of water. I never shall forget his answer. He said, "When the Lord gave me a new heart, He did not give me a new stomach. I still have the same old stomach that liquor ruined." May I say to you, "Whatever a man sows, that shall he also reap."

And this is the reason I feel so sorry for many of these kids who have been on drugs. Many of them are turning to Christ. I have received literally hundreds of letters from ex-hippies who have changed lives. But, as I told one up in the Bay area, "It's wonderful that you have come to Christ now, but when you begin to get around fifty years of age, you're going to find out that your body will have to pay for what you went through." You don't escape. You cannot escape. God says, "Whatever a man soweth, that shall he also reap."

The Fifth Reason—A High Purpose of God

There is a fifth reason God's children suffer, and that seems to be some lofty purpose of God which He does not always reveal to the believer. Job is an example of this. I am inclined to believe that Job wrote the book that bears his name, and I wonder if Job was made to suffer, not because there was anything wrong in his life, but he was made to suffer because Satan had made a spurious remark, an accusation against him and God. In substance, Satan's charge was, "Job is serving You only for what he can get out of it. If You let me get to him, I'll show You. He'll turn against You. He'll curse You to Your face!" So God then took down the hedge He had around Job and let Satan move in. And, as this man suffered, he demonstrated that he was no paid lover—that Job didn't love God for what he could get out of it. He was really genuine.

Also God said a strange thing about Paul the apostle when he was converted. He said He was going to make him a missionary to the Gentiles, then He said, "I will show him how great things he must suffer for my name's sake" (Acts 9:16). While it is true that Paul suffered for sins in his life before his conversion and he reaped what he had sown, he also suffered immeasurably in his life as a missionary. He details this in his second letter to the Corinthians:

> . . . *In labors more abundant, in stripes above measure, in prisons more frequently, in deaths often. Of the Jews five times received I forty stripes, save one. Thrice was I beaten with rods, once was I stoned, thrice I suffered shipwreck, a night and a day I have been in the deep; in journeyings often, in perils of waters, in perils of robbers, in perils by mine own countrymen, in perils by the Gentiles, in perils in the city, in perils in the wilderness, in perils in the sea, in perils among false*

brethren; in weariness and painfulness, in watchings often, in hunger and thirst, in fastings often, in cold and nakedness. Beside those things that are without, that which cometh upon me daily, the care of all the churches. (2 Corinthians 11:23–28)

He suffered so that no one can say, "Well, nobody has ever suffered as I've suffered." Paul has experienced the limit, friend. You and I never have suffered as much as he has. He is to stand as a witness to that for every child of God.

The Sixth Reason—Faith

Now we come to the sixth reason Christians suffer. Some believers suffer for their faith in a heroic manner. And this is something I noticed for the first time in Hebrews, chapter 11, as I was going through it this time. Notice the following verses:

Who, through faith, subdued kingdoms, wrought righteousness, obtained promises, stopped the mouths of lions, quenched the violence of fire, escaped the edge of the sword, out of weakness were made strong, became valiant in fight, turned to flight the armies of the aliens. Women received their dead raised to life again. . . . (Hebrews 11:33–35)

Here is a group of people who, by faith, gained great victories for God. This is wonderful. And, friend, it *is* wonderful to be able to say, "I've been healed." No one knows how happy I've been to be able to say that. But there are some who haven't been able to say that. In the middle of verse 35 we are introduced to another company. Notice what we are told about them.

. . . And others were tortured, not accepting deliverance, that they might obtain a better resurrection: and others had trial of cruel mockings and scourgings, yea, moreover, of bonds and imprisonment; they were stoned, they were sawn asunder, were tested, were

slain with the sword; they wandered about in sheep-
skins and goatskins; being destitute, afflicted, tor-
mented (of whom the world was not worthy); they wan-
dered in deserts, and in mountains, and in dens and
caves of the earth. (Hebrews 11:35–38)

Now this is a strange thing. We first saw a group of people
who by faith escaped the edge of the sword. Then here is
another group of people who were slain by the sword, and
both acted by faith. Frankly, I don't even propose to recon-
cile the two. There are some folk whom God permits to
suffer—you have known saints like this. I rather think they
are His choice saints. James and Peter, you recall, were
arrested by old Herod. Herod took James and put him to
death. Peter he put in prison, but God got him out. Is the
Lord playing favorites? No, He is not. James could endure
martyrdom; Peter could not at this time. Later on he was a
martyr also, but not now. He was growing in grace.

It is my opinion that God does not permit some Christians to suffer for the simple reason they can't take it. God
lets one group escape the edge of the sword, and they do it
by faith. But I don't think they had quite as much faith as
the other group had. I think of the French Huguenots (and
when France destroyed the Huguenots, that's the day the
nation started down to become a second-rate nation). The
Huguenots went into battle, knowing they would be slain,
saying, "If God be for us, who can be against us?" I don't
know that I could have joined their army. I'm a little too
flabby for that army. But they were able to do it.

The Seventh Reason—Discipline

As we come now to the seventh and last reason God's
children suffer, let us read Hebrews 12:6.

For whom the Lord loveth he chasteneth, and scourgeth
every son whom he receiveth. (Hebrews 12:6)

The word "chasten" is a bit misunderstood because it is interpreted as meaning punishment. Actually it is not that at all. It belongs in an altogether different category. It literally means child training. Our word today for it would be *discipline.* In other words, God does not have undisciplined children. He disciplines His own, and there are certain lessons He gets through to us by suffering. Therefore we have this matter of discipline. The Judge punishes; the Father chastens. Punishment is for breaking the rules of the Father, as we have seen. God deals that way with His children. But when He chastises, or child trains, He is doing that in love. It does not have the same background as punishment has. However, this does not mean it is not severe and that it does not hurt.

It's rather like the old chestnut about the father who took his son out to the woodshed for a little discipline. But before the father whipped the boy, he sat down and wept. As he looked up at the boy, he said, "Son, this hurts me more than it does you." And the son said, "Yes, Dad, but not in the same place."

Our heavenly Father, I'm confident, is not severe because He takes delight in disciplining us, but He does it for our benefit. Therefore, the writers of Scripture did not show us, as God's children, how to *escape* suffering but how to *endure* suffering. That is the most important thing. There is a worthy purpose and a productive goal to be gained in the chastening or the discipline of the Lord. God uses that method.

BENEFITS OF SUFFERING

There are several benefits that accrue to you and me through the discipline of the Lord. I want to mention four of them.

Patience

> *If ye endure chastening, God dealeth with you as with sons; for what son is he whom the father chasteneth not?* (Hebrews 12:7)

Patience means to be able to endure, to be able to endure suffering. Therefore God disciplines us in order that He may teach us how to endure trials, sickness, and suffering. Patience is one of the fruits of the Spirit. It doesn't come in a gift-wrapped package at Christmas. Patience is something that comes through suffering. In Romans, Paul says that tribulation or trouble works patience in the life of a believer:

> *. . . But we glory in tribulations also, knowing that tribulation worketh patience.* (Romans 5:3)

Again let me say that to suffer and not realize why you are suffering is, to my judgment, one of the most foolish things a believer can do. When God disciplines us, He is trying to teach us endurance. He is trying to teach us patience.

Assurance

Now the second thing He is trying to teach is proof that we are children of God. If you want real proof that you are God's child, suffering will provide that.

> *But if ye be without chastisement, of which all are partakers, then are ye bastards, and not sons.* (Hebrews 12:8)

He says here that if God does not discipline you, then you are not actually His child. God disciplines His children, every one that He receives. A proof that you are a child of God is the fact that He disciplines you. Suffering is not always an evidence that you are in disfavor with God. It is not always an evidence that you are out of His will or that you've done something wrong. Rather, it is proof positive that you are His child. He is trying to teach you something, and He is trying to show you that you are His child.

It may be that we as Americans will soon have real testings. The little changes we are having to make now in our lifestyle are nothing, in my opinion, to what may be coming in the future. And it may be a marvelous way God will use of weeding out those who are not His own.

William the Conqueror, who probably did more for England than any other ruler (in that he is the one who tore down the old Saxon buildings of wood and began to erect those magnificent structures like Westminster Abbey and St. John's Chapel, which is in the Tower of London), is called William the Conqueror, but he didn't sign his name that way. He signed his name William the Bastard because he was the illegitimate son of Robert, Duke of Normandy, and was recognized by Robert to succeed in his place. And so William the Conqueror never let the world forget his real background. I believe that a great many church members today could sign their names the same way. They are church members, but they actually are not children of God. They really haven't been born again into the family of God. They have no proof that they are God's children.

God disciplines His own so that we will *know* we belong to Him.

Profit

There is a third reason for God's discipline. It is for our profit.

Furthermore, we have had fathers of our flesh who corrected us, and we gave them reverence. Shall we not much rather be in subjection unto the Father of spirits, and live? For they verily for a few days chastened us after their own pleasure, but he for our profit, that we might be partakers of his holiness. (Hebrews 12:9–10)

The "profit" here is not material profit. I don't think that book I mentioned which claims to show how you can make a million dollars by becoming a Christian ought to be in print. I do not think God is moving in that direction today. The profit happens to be spiritual profit, and that is "partakers of his holiness."

You and I live in a day of action, which also is in the church. I've said many times, "Get busy for God. Do something for God." And we have a great deal of activity and movement instead of a desire to live a holy life for God. But He wants a holy life. He wants that above your service. Really, what has happened to old-fashioned holiness? I started off in the Methodist church, and I just can't get away from it. I remember hearing Bishop Moore, of the old Southern Methodist Church, say years ago, "If the Methodists were as afraid of sin as they are of holiness, it would be a great day." Well, not only Methodists, but that would apply, I think, to believers everywhere today. We need holy living, and God disciplines His children that they might have a holy life.

Productivity

The fourth thing, and the last I shall mention, is that God wants us to be productive Christians.

> *Wherefore, lift up the hands which hang down, and the feeble knees; and make straight paths for your feet, lest that which is lame be turned out of the way; but let it rather be healed.* (Hebrews 12:12–13)

In other words, God wants us to grow up. He wants to get us off pablum and out of the baby stage. He wants to get us out of the spiritual nursery and get us going. He wants to make us men and women of conviction and courage, stamina and strength.

Someone asks, "How may I teach my children to live the Christian life and to attend church?" The answer is: By living the Christian life yourself and going to church yourself. This is something that is desperately needed—courage and conviction in the lives of believers.

It was my privilege to have the poet, Martha Snell Nicholson as a member of the Church of the Open Door when I was pastor in Los Angeles. She wanted to be baptized by immersion, and I baptized her in a bathtub. She was a shut-in for many years, and her body couldn't be touched anywhere without her screaming. As I baptized her, lowering her down into the tub, she screamed at the top of her voice. It was horrible. However, in spite of her suffering, the last book of poems which she wrote—she sent me a copy of it—was entitled *Hearts Held High*. Isn't that lovely? In reading any poem in that book, you would never dream that the author was suffering so. I tell you, God disciplined her in order that she might write wonderful poetry which has blessed many a heart.

The greatest pulpits in Southern California are not in churches; they are on beds of pain. There are many wonderful saints of God who are not in churches—they are not able to attend services. That is one thing the radio ministry has opened to my eyes that I'd never really seen before, the number of people in this country who are bedfast, and by faith they are living for God. I know one woman who writes a volume of letters every month to encourage missionaries on the field, and she is lying on a bed in constant pain. What a message!

REACTION TO SUFFERING

Now what is your reaction to the chastening of the Lord? How do you respond to it?

There are several ways you can react. You can despise it. That's what the writer to the Hebrews says, "Despise not thou the chastening of the Lord." Now, how can you despise it? You can despise it by ignoring it, that is, by not relating it to the fact that God is trying to get a message through to you, trying to tell you something. You can accept it just like a dumb animal or a brute beast accepts pain. And a great many people are doing this. They say, "Well, it's just my luck." My friend, if you are a child of God, you haven't had hard luck. God is trying to tell you something. He says, "Despise not thou the chastening of the Lord, nor faint when thou art rebuked of him."

Another way you can react to God's discipline is to become a crybaby. You can say, "Why did God let this happen to me?" Have you ever heard a Christian say that? He says here, "Faint not when you're rebuked of Him." That suffering, that problem, or whatever it is that has come to you, is a challenge, and God intends for it to be that.

Then there are others who become super-pious saints. They are very passive about suffering. They develop sort of a martyr complex, and they say, "Well, this is my cross and I'll bear it," when all the time there is inner rebellion going on. But they take it like the fakir in India who lies down on a board filled with nails. Oh, my friend, that is not what God wants you to do. Listen to Him:

Now no chastening for the present seemeth to be joyous, but grievous; nevertheless, afterward it yieldeth the peaceable fruit of righteousness unto them who are exercised by it. (Hebrews 12:11)

No suffering at the time seems to be pleasant. I scream at the top of my voice, if you want to know the truth, when it comes to me. Of course it is not joyous—but it's just for a brief moment. It is like the deacon in the black church in the South expressed it. The preacher had asked for verses of Scripture that were favorites. And this deacon got up and said, "My favorite verse is, 'And it came to pass.'"

Everyone looked puzzled. The preacher asked, "What do you mean your favorite verse is, 'And it came to pass'?"

"Well," he said, "when trouble comes to me, I jest turns

to where it says, 'It came to pass,' and I thank the Lord it came to pass and it didn't come to stay."

Now this may not be a correct interpretation of that Scripture, but I tell you, it's a marvelous truth which God's Word teaches. And that is what verse 11 is saying. "No chastening for the moment is joyous"—it's terrible. Don't say you are a martyr and you are going to bear it. Say, "I'm going to get out of this as quickly as I can."

Mrs. Siewert, who was responsible for the *Amplified Bible,* carried on with me a running, friendly war as long as she was alive. I would correct her Bible; then she would correct my sermons at the Church of the Open Door. When I had surgery for cancer, I asked everybody to pray for me. She wrote to me and said, "Now, Dr. McGee, you are ready to go so I am going to pray that the Lord will take you home." I wrote a reply to Mrs. Siewert in a hurry, "Don't you pray that prayer. This is between the Lord and me, and you let Him handle it." I wanted to be cured of cancer. I was prepared to learn the lesson God had for me, but I wanted to *live.* In my opinion, it is nonsense to be passive about it.

There is a fourth way we can react to suffering. We are told to endure chastening.

> *If ye endure chastening, God dealeth with you as with sons; for what son is he whom the father chasteneth not?* (Hebrews 12:7)

The thing that is important here is that we are to endure chastening. Let me be personal at this point.

When I got cancer in 1965, I made the announcement of it on my radio program, and I asked folk to pray for me. God did hear and He did answer. I had periodic x-rays made, and they showed that my lungs are still clear of the seven cancer spots. They are gone. And I thank God for healing. But I want to say this to you: I accepted cancer as punishment from God. I believe He was punishing me.

And I'll tell you the reason. I had been at the Church of the Open Door for fifteen years. I had come to the place that I didn't need the Lord to bring the crowds. I was doing it myself—I *thought* I was. As a result, the Lord put me flat on my back to let me know that I was absolutely nothing. He said, "I can remove you from this scene, and I do not need you." He punished. That was eight years ago.

Now this summer when I was stricken with an illness, I did not feel that it was punishment. I felt He was chastening me. It was discipline. I was confident that I was in God's will. I went to Him and said, "Look, I think I've learned all the lessons I need to learn, and I'd appreciate it if You would make it possible for me to fulfill my obligations." You see, I'd been going to the Northwest for twenty-five years for conferences, and I was scheduled to be up there six weeks during the summer. I didn't know what they would do without me. So I begged the Lord, "Let me go." Actually I rebelled against the chastening and against my doctor's orders. I got up and attempted to make a move. And He slapped me down, oh, so hard! I never have suffered like I suffered at that time. I had to cancel twelve conferences in the summer and fall. God assured me, "It's all right. They will get along without you. I want you to lie down and just get acquainted with Me. I want you to know that I love you and that you have a lot of lessons to learn yet." I found out that the Lord had a lot of things to teach me. I had never been brought as close to the Lord as I was during that time. Never. How wonderful He was.

When the summer was over, I got a telephone call from the Northwest about coming up next summer (which I hope I can do), and I asked them, "By the way, what kind of a summer did you have this year?" They said, "We had the best summer we have had in twenty-five years!" To the Lord I said, "They did get along without me, didn't they!" He said, "Yes. I'd like you to get acquainted with Me."

Not only that, but my wife and I sat for three months out on our patio this summer. I hate being idle. Although I did a lot of study, I wanted to make tapes and do other things. But instead I got acquainted with my wife. I was telling my doctor about it. He's a wonderful Christian but he's a little hard-boiled. He said, "Yes, and I bet you found out you have the most wonderful wife in the world." I said, "That's exactly what I found out." It's amazing what you can learn when you are flat on your back. You simply have to look up to the Lord and let Him speak to you.

How do you respond, friend, when suffering comes?

There are no accidents in a Christian's life. Even when he has an "accident," it's not accidental. It did not happen by chance. Do you take an inventory of your life when trouble comes? Do you ever evaluate your suffering? Do you turn your stumbling blocks into stepping stones?

"Why did God let this happen to me?" is a good question. And there is a better answer to it. There's a goal to be attained, a race to be won, a battle to be fought, and there is a benefit here and now.

Job discovered this truth. He says,

> *But he knoweth the way that I take; when he hath tested me, I shall come forth as gold.* (Job 23:10)

God not only refined him, but He doubled everything he had lost. Someone counters, "But God didn't double his children. He gave him the same number of children that he had lost." No, He doubled them also. You see, when he lost the cattle, he lost them permanently—they were gone forever. But when he lost his children, he did not actually lose them—they just went on before him. So God *doubled* his children also.

Then there is Paul the apostle. I don't read that Paul ever received a reward down here. In fact, he became a martyr, but he could say at the end of his life:

> *I have fought a good fight, I have finished my course, I have kept the faith; henceforth there is laid up for me a*

crown of righteousness, which the Lord, the righteous judge, shall give me at that day; and not to me only, but unto all them also that love his appearing. (2 Timothy 4:7–8)

Paul will get his reward afterward.

Whether now or later, there is always a reward for His faithful children. Someday God will wipe away all tears, and He will heal all the broken hearts. Then He will reveal the reasons for those puzzling experiences that you and I had down here.

Do you remember when the children of Israel went through the wilderness? They crossed the Red Sea in great victory, and they sang the song of Moses unto the Lord (Exodus 15). God delivered them. What a victory it was! Immediately their first experience in the wilderness was that of running out of water. Then they came to Marah where there was water, but when they got down to drink it, the water was bitter. They began to complain—their first experience was a bitter experience. So God said to Moses, "There is a certain tree here, you get that and put it in the water, and it will be sweet." Friend, you and I need to bring Jesus Christ and His death on the tree into the bitter experiences of our life to make them sweet. That is the only thing in the world that can make the experiences of suffering down here sweet.

We are to run with patience the race that is set before us. How?

Looking unto Jesus, the author and finisher [architect] *of our faith, who for the joy that was set before him endured the cross, despising the shame, and is set down at the right hand of the throne of God.* (Hebrews 12:2)

The most important thing is to draw near to God. When we do, He promises to draw near to us. We need to keep very close to Him in these days.

Let me conclude with a very homely illustration. When I was a boy, I went to grade school in southern Oklahoma. On April Fool's Day it was the custom among the bad boys to play hookey. Well, although I was a good boy (you could have asked my mother and she would have told you what a fine boy I was!), I went with a bad crowd. On April Fool's Day I would play hookey with these boys. Well, one time we came to school on April the first, put our books in our desks, then about a dozen of us went down to the old Phillip's Creek to go fishing. It wasn't a good time to fish because it was the spring of the year and the water in the creeks was at a high level. Fish just don't bite when the creeks are up. But we fished nonetheless and had a good time running up and down the creek to the different holes we knew. None of us caught any fish, but we had a great day. When we started back home, the problems began to arise. We decided the best thing to do was to go by the school, get our books and take them home so our parents would not suspect what we had done. When we reached the schoolhouse, everybody had gone, so we walked into our room. And when we walked into the room, the principal, apparently knowing what we would do, walked in after us.

"Boys, did you have a good day?"

"Yes, sir." It *had* been a good day up to that moment!

"Did you catch any fish?"

"No."

"Well, follow me," he instructed. And he began a parade down the hallway to his office. He sat us down and gave us a little talk. We knew what was coming. He said, "Now I keep my switches down the hallway locked up in a closet. I'll go down and get them, and I'll come back and punish each one of you."

So while he was gone to get his switches, one of the boys, who had been in there more than any of the rest of us had and knew his way around, gave the best advice that I ever received. He said, "Now when he hits you with that switch, the first lick will just burn you up because he starts off with you way out on the end of the switch. But as he whips you, take a step toward him. Keep moving toward him. The closer you get to him, the less it'll hurt."

That was the best advice I ever had. I remember the first lick he hit me. It really burned. But I began to edge toward him, and when he finished, I was somewhere pretty close to his hand and it wasn't hurting me at all.

That was a great lesson. And since then, I have learned that God also disciplines His children. If you don't want it to hurt, the thing to do is to get close to Him. The closer you are, the less it will hurt.

You remember that the Lord Jesus said (as recorded in John 15) that He is the vine, we are the branches, and the Father prunes the branches. That hurts to be trimmed like that! But, as the old Scotch divine said, the Father is never so close to the branches as when He is trimming them. That is wonderful. We need to get close and stay close to Him.

The following lovely little poem was given to me when I had cancer surgery and again during my latest illness. I have deeply appreciated it, and I'd like to share it with you.

I Needed the Quiet

I needed the quiet so He drew me aside,
Into the shadows where we could confide.
Away from the bustle where all the day long
I hurried and worried when active and strong.
I needed the quiet though at first I rebelled,
But gently, so gently, my cross He upheld,
And whispered so sweetly of spiritual things.
Though weakened in body, my spirit took wings
To heights never dreamed of when active and gay.
He loved me so greatly He drew me away.
I needed the quiet. No prison my bed,

But a beautiful valley of blessings instead—
A place to grow richer in Jesus to hide.
I needed the quiet so He drew me aside.

—Alice Hansche Mortenson

12

THREE WORLDS IN ONE

(2 Peter 3)

The three worlds in one—the world that *was*, the world that *is*, and the world that *will be*—are described for us in the third chapter of Peter's second letter:

This second epistle, beloved, I now write unto you, in both of which I stir up your pure minds by way of remembrance, that ye may be mindful of the words which were spoken before by the holy prophets, and of the commandment of us, the apostles of the Lord and Savior; knowing this first, that there shall come in the last days scoffers, walking after their own lusts, and saying, Where is the promise of his coming? For since the fathers fell asleep, all things continue as they were from the beginning of the creation. For this they willingly are ignorant of, that by the word of God the heavens were of old, and the earth standing out of the water and in the water, by which the world that then was, being over-flowed with water, perished. But the heavens and the earth which are now, by the same word are kept in store, reserved unto fire against the day of judgment and perdition of ungodly men. But, beloved, be not ignorant of this one thing, that one day is with the Lord as a thousand years, and a thousand years as one day. The Lord is not slack concerning his promise, as some men count slackness, but is long-suffering toward us, not

*willing that any should perish, but that all should come
to repentance. But the day of the Lord will come as a
thief in the night, in which the heavens shall pass away
with a great noise, and the elements shall melt with
fervent heat; the earth also, and the works that are in it,
shall be burned up. Seeing, then, that all these things
shall be dissolved, what manner of persons ought ye to
be in all holy living and godliness, looking for and hast-
ing unto the coming of the day of God, in which the
heavens, being on fire, shall be dissolved, and the elements shall melt with fervent heat? Nevertheless we,
according to his promise, look for new heavens and a
new earth, in which dwelleth righteousness. Wherefore,
beloved, seeing that ye look for such things, be diligent
that ye may be found of him in peace, without spot, and
blameless. And account that the long-suffering of our
Lord is salvation, even as our beloved brother, Paul,
also according to the wisdom given unto him hath written unto you; as also in all his epistles, speaking in
them of these things, in which are some things hard to
be understood, which they that are unlearned and unstable wrest, as they do also the other scriptures, unto
their own destruction. Ye therefore, beloved, seeing that
ye know these things before, beware lest ye also, being
led away with the error of the wicked, fall from your
own steadfastness. But grow in grace, and in the
knowledge of our Lord and Savior, Jesus Christ. To him
be glory both now and forever. Amen.* (2 Peter 3)

Surely we have all been impressed in the past with the
advertising of a certain shoe polish which boasts of its
product as a "two-in-one" article. We have also noted the
claims of a sewing machine oil which goes the shoe polish
one better by saying it is a "three-in-one" product. Nevertheless, I dare say that most of us have never realized that
we live in a three-in-one world. That is the exact thought in
this third chapter of 2 Peter. It is rather three periods of
time that we have here. I should like to identify these three
worlds.

THE WORLD THAT WAS

The first one is mentioned in verses 5 and 6:

For this they willingly are ignorant of, that by the word of God the heavens were of old, and the earth standing out of the water and in the water, by which the world that then was, being overflowed with water, perished.

That is the "world that was."

In verse 7 we have our next reference:

But the heavens and the earth which are now, by the same word are kept in store, reserved unto fire against the day of judgment and perdition of ungodly men.

This is the present world or the "world that is."

And then we have the third world mentioned in verse 13:

Nevertheless we, according to his promise, look for new heavens and a new earth, in which dwelleth righteousness.

And this is the "world that will be." Actually, we have here only one world but three periods of time: The world of the past, the world of the present, and the world of the future.

One World

Now we have been introduced in our generation to the one-world idea, and it has been presented to us as something entirely new. When Wendell Willkie toured around the world and returned to write his book, *One World,* that was probably the first time that this idea was made available for public consumption. At least, it is the first time it came into the limelight for John Q. Public to consider. And the flash of the atomic bomb crystallized this thought to such an extent that after World War II the public demanded an adequate answer to meet this new need of the

one-world idea. The United Nations was man's answer to
meet this new problem—and let us be very clear, it was
man's answer and not God's. Many world-wide movements have come into focus since then, and we hear a great
deal today about global politics. But, you know, this is not
something new. We have had ecumenical movements in the
church for many years. Nevertheless, all of this caused us
to coin new mottoes, and we heard new phrases: Unite or
Perish, Federate or Disintegrate, Yoke Up or Blow Up.
Now these are not God's movements, and certainly they
are not His solutions to the problem. But God does have a
global gospel today that was meant for every race and tribe
and tongue and nation on top side of this earth. The fact of
the matter is that this gospel is going to reach all of these
because the day is coming when there will be gathered in
His presence out of every nation, tribe, tongue, and condition of mankind those that have been redeemed by this
glorious gospel. But this one-world idea—it is about two
thousand years old.

Let us look at verses 3 and 4 of 2 Peter 3 and we shall see
in it the expression, "the world that was":

> *Knowing this first, that there shall come in the last days
> scoffers, walking after their own lusts, and saying,
> Where is the promise of his coming? For since the fa-
> thers fell asleep, all things continue as they were from
> the beginning of the creation.*

You see, scoffers were to arise who would ridicule the notion that the Lord Jesus Christ would return. And they
present a very specious argument, an argument which lacks
logic and has no foundation in fact. They say, "Where is
the promise of His coming? For since the fathers fell
asleep, all things continue as they were from the beginning
of the creation." They, of course, want to adopt the doctrine of *laissez faire,* and they are willing to continue the
status quo because they believe that everything has contin-

ued on an even tempo from the very beginning. That may have sounded plausible in Peter's day, and it may sound plausible to some now. But surely it is not true to the facts as we know them today because there was a world that came into judgment, and that world perished. This is the statement we have in verse 6:

> *By which the world that then was, being overflowed with water, perished.*

There was a judgment of this world in the past, you see; the world that then existed perished.

Scar Marks of the Water Judgment Upon the Earth

The very interesting thing is that both the heavens and the earth bear scar marks of a past judgment. That is the subject of common knowledge today, and it is needless for me to go into a great many details. However, I would like to mention a few:

We know today that the mountains, especially out here in the western country, have been thrown up by some major catastrophe of the past. I well recall my first trip to Yosemite Valley, listening to the ranger there give his memorized lecture that evidently had been handed to him by some geologist. This ranger made the statement that sometime in the ages past there was a colossal glacier that moved down through that area, cutting out the mighty Yosemite Valley. My, what a chiseler it took to perform such a feat!

Another evidence is found in the presence of seashells on mountain tops. I was speaking several years ago to an oil geologist in Texas—a very fine Christian, by the way—and I was telling him of an experience I had had while squirrel hunting down near the Brazos River. Along the river bank I had noted a strata of rock with nothing but dirt beneath it and nothing but dirt above it. On closer examination of that strata of rock, I found out that it was nothing in the world but crushed seashells cemented together. The geologist made this statement, "It is quite evident that this entire state as well as this western area was at one time under water."

And we are all familiar, I am sure, with the account of the animals which have been found in Siberia in "deep freeze." They have been there through the centuries. Elephants, for instance, have been found with grass in their stomachs—green grass. They evidently were enjoying a tropical climate in that area when all of a sudden, through some major catastrophe, they were put in quick freeze.

In other words, the laws of nature as we know them today were interrupted; something interfered, the *status quo* was disturbed, and a mighty cataclysm came upon this earth. In fact, "cataclysm" is the very word that Peter uses, and he says it was a judgment by water. At that time a great inundation took place which submerged the civilization of that day beneath watery waves.

In the world as we know it today, three-fourths of its surface is water. It is one of the basic materials. Even the Greek philosophers from the very beginning always considered water one of the basic materials. Thales, an early Greek philosopher, speaks of four basic elements: water, fire, air, and earth. And we know that this water was the destructive force. In other words, there is resident in nature its own destructive force, and there was a judgment of God upon the world at that time by water.

God's Judgment, Not Love, Manifest in Nature

As you look out today at the world of nature, you will not discover the love of God, for the love of God is not revealed in nature at all. You will not find the love of God, as the poets like to speak of it, in the birds and bees and the budding of the trees. Nature today has a bloody tooth and a very sharp claw. As I write, the great drifts of snow out in the Middle West have caused farmers to be isolated and have not only endangered life but actually have caused many to die. The forces of nature which are at work today do not reveal God's love.

You will not find the love of God today except in one place, and that is in the cross of Jesus Christ. It is there God has made the focal point for all His love, and there He showered all His mercy. And if you are to know the love of God, you will have to find it at the cross where He gave His Son to die for you.

The heavens, likewise, bear scar marks of a judgment of the past. I have been very much interested in reading a book by an astronomer concerning the dark nebuli. He holds that these dark nebuli are evidently stellar systems like our Milky Way that are out yonder beyond our galaxy. By the way, these dark spots in the sky are not dark at all, for beyond them there are stars. It is supposed that these dark spots have been caused by some sort of a major catastrophe which took place in the past. Surely new telescopes will flood this subject with new light. Until then, I will have to reserve my opinion relative to this.

The Time of the Water Judgment

Now the question arises: When did this judgment which produced the flood take place on the earth? Let me quote again to you verses 5 and 6 of 2 Peter 3:

> *For this they willingly are ignorant of, that by the word of God the heavens were of old, and the earth standing out of the water and in the water, by which the world that then was, being overflowed with water, perished.*

It is impossible for us to date the great catastrophe when the world was destroyed by water. There are, however, two possibilities:

The Flood of Noah's Day. I have asked several outstanding Bible teachers what judgment they thought Peter had in mind, and there was some disagreement among these men. Most of them did agree, however, that it referred to the flood of Noah's day. Surely that seems to be the suggestion here.

The antediluvian civilization was destroyed with a flood, and there is abundant evidence for this. The great shaft which was put down at the site of ancient Ur of the Chaldees shows that there were several civilizations destroyed. In the excavation, the archaeologists came to a great deal of sand and silt and quite a bit of sediment that was deposited there by a flood. Then beneath all this, they found that a very high civilization had existed. Personally, I believe that Peter referred directly to the flood of Noah's day, and surely this earth bears abundant evidence of this flood.

The Judgment of the Pre-Adamic World. There was another judgment concerning which we know very little, and this judgment took place in the pre-Adamic world. It is suggested in the very first few verses of the Bible. In Genesis 1:1,2 we read:

> *In the beginning God created the heaven and the earth. And the earth was without form, and void; and darkness was upon the face of the deep. And the Spirit of God moved* [brooded] *upon the face of the waters.*

God created the heavens and the earth, and then we find the earth without form and void, or better still, "It *became* without form, and void."

The literal translation is that it became *tohu-wa-bohu.* In Isaiah 45:18 the prophet says that God did not create this world *tohu-wa-bohu,* which would suggest that something happened that made this world without form and void. In other words, a cataclysm came upon this earth. When God began to move, water was upon the face of this earth. One of the first things that God had to do, after He brought light, was to remove the water from the land and to separate the land from the water.

The view I hold is that there was a great judgment that took place in this pre-Adamic civilization. We know practically nothing about it although it seems that this judgment is in connection with the fall of Satan who was created Lucifer, "the son of the morning," an "angel of light," evidently the very highest creature that God ever created. And we find this mentioned in Isaiah 14:12–14:

> *How art thou fallen from heaven, O Lucifer, son of the morning! How art thou cut down to the ground, who didst weaken the nations! For thou hast said in thine heart, I will ascend into heaven, I will exalt my throne above the stars of God; I will sit also upon the mount of the congregation, in the sides of the north, I will ascend above the heights of the clouds, I will be like the Most High.*

We have here what was evidently the origin of sin. Sin, here at the very beginning, is connected with the fall of Lucifer. This one, created so high, lifted his will against the will of God. In other words, there was rebellion in heaven against God. And, my friends, this is sin at its very core. I suppose the worst thing that can be said about any man is that which is recorded in Isaiah 53 where it is said that each one has turned to "his own way." That is, we set *our way* over against *the way of God*. That is sin in its inception; that is sin at its blackest; that is sin in its origin. The way all sins begin is by man setting his will over against the will of God. And here we find this creature, the highest creature that God ever created, setting his will over against the will of God. He did not say he would be unlike God, that he wanted to be different from God. He said, "I want to be like God." And he tried to lift himself up and set himself up as God and set his will over against the will of God. And that is what rebellious man is doing today. He is setting himself up as his own little god or insisting on his own particular viewpoint of God. Each one is turned to his own way.

This judgment in 2 Peter could refer to this pre-Adamic civilization in which Satan, who evidently at that time was Lucifer, an angel of light, had control. When he rebelled and set his will over against God, then the judgment of God came upon this earth. And it was a water judgment.

God's Messengers to This Present World

God has judged sin in the past. This earth bears scar marks, open wounds that testify that God has moved in mighty judgment against that which opposed Him. And since He has judged sin in the past, He is going to judge sin in the future. You are living in a world that is on its way to destruction. We are going to deal with that in the next section. This world in which we are living today is moving toward a judgment, not by flood, because there hangs over this earth the rainbow of many hues and colors, the rainbow of the grace and patience of God, but the judgment of God is coming. This world will be destroyed. Every time you pick up a popular magazine and read a scientific article about prehistoric creatures who existed upon this earth thousands, even millions, of years ago—for that is quite possible—God is speaking to your heart to let you know that a judgment came upon that civilization because it had turned its back upon God.

God is speaking today; He is speaking to men and women in all walks of life and in many ways. In effect He is saying to them, "In view of the fact that I have judged sin in the past, don't you know that I am going to judge sin in the future?" That is the message which He is trying to get over to this gainsaying world today that seems so dull of hearing and filled with scoffers.

God speaks in many ways. I believe that the snowstorms, floods, and droughts are a judgment from God. I believe that He is using them to speak to America. The dust storms that we had during the Depression, as so many of God's messengers at that time pointed out, were God's warning to America. At that time there was no revival, no turning back to God; but I do believe that if America had heeded God and turned back to Him, we would not have had to send our boys to die in the second World War and on battlefields all over the world.

God also speaks to men personally. The very gray in your hair, the rheumatism and the difficulty that you are having in your physical body—all of these are just messages from God to let you know that you are not going to be in this world too much longer. Signs of aging are merely God's messengers, telling you that you are to be removed from this place. You see, God is not going to take you out in a hurry; He gives you plenty of warning. But having given you the warning, He then moves in.

You will recall that Noah preached one hundred and twenty years, and certainly that was long enough to give the people of that day an ample opportunity to decide whether they would turn to God or not. The Lord Jesus, speaking of that in Matthew 24:37–38, said:

> *But as the days of Noah were, so shall also the coming of the Son of man be. . . . They were eating and drinking, marrying and giving in marriage, until the day that Noah entered into the ark.*

Now is there anything wrong with eating and drinking? Is there anything wrong with marrying and giving in marriage? Certainly not. Then why did the Lord Jesus mention those things? The reason He mentioned them is that after Noah had preached one hundred and twenty years, telling them of the imminent danger they were in, they were going through these ordinary pursuits of life, such as eating and drinking, marrying and giving in marriage, and were paying no attention to the fact that the flood was even then at their doors. God was warning them, and the thing that was wrong was that they were not listening to His messenger at all.

I know that there are many of you who think this sounds old-fashioned—and certainly it is—because in the years gone by God's messengers had a great deal to say about the judgment of God. And you probably think that I drive around in a Stanley Steamer since I am such a back number in mentioning these things. Or you may think that I am attempting to frighten you. Do not think that. I know that we live in a skeptical and sophisticated age, and I have too much respect for your intelligence to believe that I can frighten you. But, my friend, you and I are living in a world that is moving to judgment. The reason we know it is moving to judgment is that God has judged sin in the past, and certainly sin is prevalent today. No civilization has gotten by with it; eventually God is going to move in judgment.

Let me share with you this little story that came to my attention several years ago while I was doing graduate work in the Dallas Seminary. I was walking down the main street in Dallas one evening after dinner with another student. We noticed a crowd in front of a theater gathered around an automobile that had been in a wreck. The fact of the matter is that I have never seen an automobile that was so completely wrecked. We were told that the passengers had been killed and that their bodies had to be sawed out of that car because they were so tightly locked in it. Upon returning to the seminary, we were telling the fellows there what we had seen. One of them told us this story, for he knew all about it. He taught a Bible class in one of the suburban communities of Dallas, and in that Bible class were quite a few high school students, some of whom had been converted, including several on the football team. However, others had become very skeptical and were ridiculing the Christians. Two boys and a girl went by to get one of the girls that formerly had been running with this crowd. She told them that she would not go with them but that she was going to a Bible class that evening instead, and she tried to persuade them to go. Well, they merely laughed and went on their way. And so every Monday evening they would come by and try to get her to ditch the Bible class and go with them. She tried to plead with them to accept Christ as their Savior; she told them what she had done and the step she had taken. One Monday night they asked if they might take her by the Bible class, which they did. When they let her out, she pleaded with them again to come in just one time. Refusing, they started out in their car again. They had not gone two miles until the accident took place that killed all three of them. This was the car that was there in front of the theater which we had seen.

You know, God is gracious, but after He has given us His message and we turn our backs upon it, there is nothing left but His judgment. Oh! that you and I might be warned to turn to Him while it is called "today"; "now is the accepted time."

THE WORLD THAT IS

As we come to the "world that is," I am turning to the Revised Standard Version, reading this chapter over again. It is not that I recommend this version, but I am very much interested in getting at the meaning of some words, and it is well to note the difference from our Authorized translation and any other translation of the Scriptures.

This is now the second letter that I have written to you, beloved, and in both of them I have aroused your sincere mind by way of reminder; that you should remember the predictions of the holy prophets and the commandment of the Lord and Savior through your apostles. First of all you must understand this, that scoffers will come in the last days with scoffing, following their own passions and saying, "Where is the promise of his coming? For ever since the fathers fell asleep, all things have continued as they were from the beginning of creation." They deliberately ignore this fact, that by the word of God heavens existed long ago, and an earth formed out of water and by means of water, through which the world that then existed was deluged with water and perished. But by the same word the heavens and earth that now exist have been stored up for fire, being kept until the day of judgment and destruction of ungodly men.

But do not ignore this one fact, beloved, that with the Lord one day is as a thousand years, and a thousand years as one day. The Lord is not slow about his promise as some count slowness, but is forbearing toward you, not wishing that any should perish, but that all should reach repentance. But the day of the Lord will come like a thief, and then the heavens will pass away with a loud noise, and the elements will be dissolved with fire, and the earth and the works that are upon it will be burned up.

Since all these things are thus to be dissolved, what sort of persons ought you to be in lives of holiness and godliness, waiting for and hastening the coming of the day of God, because of which the heavens will be kindled and dissolved, and the elements will melt with fire! But according to his promise we wait for new heavens and a new earth in which righteousness dwells.

Therefore, beloved, since you wait for these, be zealous to be found by him without spot or blemish, and at peace. And count the forbearance of our Lord as salvation. So also our beloved brother Paul wrote to you according to the wisdom given him, speaking of this as he does in all his letters. There are some things in them hard to understand, which the ignorant and unstable twist to their own destruction, as they do the other scriptures. You therefore, beloved, knowing this beforehand, beware lest you be carried away with the error of lawless men and lose your own stability. But grow in the grace and knowledge of our Lord and Savior Jesus Christ. To him be the glory both now and to the day of eternity. Amen. (2 Peter 3, RSV)

False Premises Concerning the Lord's Second Coming

The reason that Peter mentions "the world that was," "the world that is," and "the world that will be" is due to the fact that in the last days scoffers will arise, and they will ridicule the truth concerning the coming of Christ again to this earth. The scoffers in the past based their ridicule on two false premises:

Nothing has happened in the past; therefore, nothing will happen in the future. They base their ridicule on the false assumption that since nothing has happened in the past, nothing will happen in the future. I say it is a false assumption, a counterfeit premise, because, as we have seen, something *has* happened in the past. This world bears scar marks of a past judgment; the very stones cry out, telling the story of a past civilization that was submerged beneath water. They tell us that the cosmos that was then in existence was brought into chaos and that this present world in which we are living today is built on that chaos. There is every evidence of that, of course.

Before we go on to the second false premise on which scoffers in this present world base their belief that the Lord will not return, I should like to answer some questions which naturally arise in connection with the destruction of this present world: Will it be drowned? Will it be drenched? Will it be put beneath the flood? Verses 7, 10, and 12 answer these questions, and in these three verses we find it definitely stated that the present world will be destroyed by fire, not by water. Let us note, first of all, verse 7:

> *But by the same word the heavens and earth that now exist have been stored up for fire, being kept until the day of judgment and destruction of ungodly men.*

This present order of things is temporary. This present world in which we are living today is moving toward another day of judgment, which is unlike anything in the past.

This time it is a judgment by fire. In fact, Peter is very specific in this epistle and in this particular passage, mentioning it three times (verses 7, 10 and 12).

Now let us look at verse 10:

> *But the day of the Lord will come like a thief, and then the heavens will pass away with a loud noise, and the elements will be dissolved with fire, and the earth and the works that are upon it will be burned up.*

There you see that Peter not only says that this world will be "dissolved with fire," but also that it will be "burned up." How could he be more specific?

The third reference is as follows, in verse 12:

> *Waiting for and hastening the coming of the day of God, because of which the heavens will be kindled and dissolved, and the elements will melt with fire!*

This is one of the most remarkable passages in the Word of God, especially for the present hour. It is this passage of Scripture which has caused the skeptic of the past to ridicule. If you should consider many of the criticisms that have been made in past ages, one that caused the loudest guffaws was the question: "How can water burn? Most of the world today is water, and it is ridiculous to think that it can burn." Of course at the present hour that sort of criticism is outmoded because we know today that water is made of two inflammable gases and that it can burn.

Now let us return to the second false premise mentioned above: *the eternity of matter.* This was a premise on which a great deal of the science of the past was based, something which was taught by Plato. You see, they said this passage could never come to pass because matter was indestructible and could not be destroyed; matter was eternal. Not only did the critics ridicule this passage, but also the Bible scholars of the past were puzzled by it. Though they believed it sincerely and humbly, they could not explain it. And I have been very much interested in noting that some of them felt called upon to make some sort of an explanation, one saying that probably this earth will bump into some other heavenly body causing a mighty conflagration. That could be, of course, but it does not seem likely with the information that has come to us and since we know that the thing that is mentioned here in this third chapter of 2 Peter can happen. We not only know that it can happen, but we also know *how* it can happen. When the atomic bomb fell on Hiroshima, a flood of light fell on this chapter. The fact of the matter is that this is the only good that the atomic bomb has done so far. It has at least given us a commentary on 2 Peter 3.

Atomic Fission Explains the Language of Peter

In atomic fission (when the little atom is split) the tremendous force that is released consumes it. I want us to note the language very definitely in the three verses previously quoted. They speak of the fact that this present order of things will be destroyed by fire. Therefore, let us return to verses 7, 10, and 12, taking them in chronological order, continuing with the Revised Standard Version, verse 7:

> *But by the same word the heavens and earth that now exist have been stored up for fire, being kept until the day of judgment and destruction of ungodly men.*

Note that it says that this earth has been stored up for fire. This is a very interesting expression, by the way, and it not only means stored up *for* fire but also stored up *with* fire (that could easily be the translation of it). The suggestion is that there are resident forces present in the world which could destroy it. In other words, this world can commit suicide. This possibility is suggested in this passage. It is not that God is going to rain fire down from heaven—it is not that there is coming in from the outside some medium of judgment—but this earth carries its own judgment. How well we know this today! Now note verse 10:

> *But the day of the Lord will come like a thief, and then the heavens will pass away with a loud noise, and the elements will be dissolved with fire, and the earth and the works that are upon it will be burned up.*

There are several expressions here which we want to examine in detail. A loud "noise" (Greek *rhoizēdon)* is a word used by Simon Peter that is not found anywhere else in the New Testament. It is a word that belongs to classical Greek. It belongs to the poets, for the pronunciation carries its own meaning. It is sometimes used to speak of the swish of an arrow, the hiss of a serpent, or the splash of water. Does that not suggest to you the sound of atomic explosion? This is the very word and the only word that I know that could describe such a noise.

"The elements will be dissolved with fire" or "the elements shall melt," as the King James translation has it, is a very interesting expression and contains two remarkable words: *elements* and *melt.* First let us examine the word *elements.* The word for elements here means the basic materials, and it is the word used to speak of putting building blocks in a row or a series. It is used to speak of the first steps of a child. It is that which is primary, that which is foundational, that out of which a thing is made.

This is much better than our word "atom." You see, the word "atom" comes from the Greek word *tomao,* which means to cut. An *alpha* (the first letter of the Greek alphabet) gives the opposite meaning when placed at the beginning of a word. So *atomao* (atom) means something which you cannot cut. That is what scientists thought a few years ago about the atom—that it was something that could not be cut. But now it is being cut up like a railroad restaurant pie. The word translated "elements" is a much better word, for it means the basic materials. As one of the outstanding scientists of the present hour expressed it, "The atoms are the building blocks of the universe." Thus, "elements" suggests the atomic structure of the universe.

"Melt" employs one of the simplest Greek words. It is one that every student of first-year Greek uses as his model in considering all the parts of the verb. It is the verb *luō*, and this word simply means "to untie," "to unloose." That is the word translated "melt." This passage says that the atomic structure, or the atoms of the universe, will be untied. That certainly is the way we laymen would speak of atomic fission. We are told that when the little atom is untied, an atomic explosion goes off.

In verse 10, we are also told that the earth and the works are to be burned up. That is the exact language of Peter; that is the total destruction of this universe. And, of course, that is what happens when atomic fission takes place. It means the mass has been converted to energy and tremendous heat has been released. Consider verse 12:

Waiting for and hastening the coming of the day of God, because of which the heavens will be kindled and dissolved, and the elements will melt with fire!

You will note that the expression in which we are interested in verse 12 is the same expression which we considered in verse 10: "elements shall melt." However, this time we have a different word in the original for "melt." It is not the simple little word *lūo*, but it is *tēkomai*, a word that means actually "wasting away," the wasting away of nature. This could possibly suggest the effects of radioactivity when an atomic bomb goes off.

Please note that in all three of the verses under consideration, the release of intense heat is mentioned. In verse 7 Peter mentions that "the heavens and earth . . . have been stored up for *fire*" and in verse 10 that "the elements will be dissolved with *fire*" and in verse 12 that "the elements will melt with *fire*." These references certainly speak of a fervent heat that is to be generated. These are things that cannot escape even the casual reader. And the analogy to atomic action again is striking. Certainly we have here a rather interesting description of atomic fission written about two thousand years ago.

In 1947 a very interesting little brochure was printed relative to the atomic bomb and what the Bible says about it. The writer evidently went to a great deal of trouble to gather quite a lot of information regarding the experiment which was made in Alamogordo, New Mexico. He tells us that he had dinner with a Christian railroad man who lived about one hundred miles from Alamogordo. On the morning of the fateful experiment, this man was preparing breakfast at about five o'clock when suddenly the sky became so lighted up that the fluorescent fixture in his kitchen seemed as if it were dark rather than light. The writer of the book mentioned also a blind girl in Albuquerque, New Mexico, which is about one hundred and twenty miles from Alamogordo. She had been waiting on the street for a bus, and when the bomb went off, she exclaimed, "What is that?" We are told that this bomb that was released in Alamogordo weighed approximately four hundred pounds and that it was suspended from a tower built very much like an oil derrick, except that it was not built of any sheer materials but actually of railroad rails which weigh about ninety pounds to the foot. When this bomb, which was just a midget, went off, it dissolved this derrick which went up in a puff of smoke; and for a mile in every direction there was a place at least five feet deep that had been blasted out, and the rocks in the immediate vicinity had become molten.

This gives us a bird's-eye view of what an atomic bomb can and does do. It would seem that men of today have broken into God's treasure house; they have found God's secret, it appears. The fact of the matter is that this is the suggestion in verse 7:

*But by the same word the heavens and earth that now
exist have been stored up for fire, being kept until the
day of judgment and destruction of ungodly men.*

This gives the suggestion of being kept in store, and that is
the same word that the Lord Jesus used when He told of
the man who was laying up treasure. God had been laying
up this secret of how He made this universe, and it seems
that man has broken into God's secret treasure house and
stolen the secret. At least, man has opened a veritable Pandora's box, and today men are frightened.

People in All Walks of Life Are Frightened

It makes no difference which way we turn today, people
in all walks of life—scientists and statesmen, college professors and presidents—are all speaking concerning the awful
possibilities of the future, warning that a chain of atomic
fission could be set off which might destroy this universe.
In other words, it is just like living on a powder keg; we are
living on a dynamite dump; we are living on an arsenal. It
can go off. God's Word says that it *will* go off some day,
and informed men of today know that to be true.

Knowledgeable people have been saying some very interesting things about this present hour. Please note that I am
not quoting from any preachers but from outstanding people in other walks of life.

Dr. Urey from the University of Chicago, who worked
on the atomic bomb, began an article several years ago in
Collier's magazine by saying, "I am a frightened man, and I
want to frighten you."

Dr. John R. Mott returned from a trip around the world
and made the statement that this was "the most dangerous
era the world has ever known." And he raised the question
of where we are heading. Then he made this further statement, "When I think of human tragedy, as I saw it and felt
it, of the Christian ideals sacrificed as they have been, the

thought comes to me that *God is preparing the way for some immense direct action.*"

Chancellor Robert M. Hutchins, of the University of Chicago, gave many people a shock several years ago when he made the statement that "devoting our educational efforts to infants between six and twenty-one seems futile." And he added, "The world may not last long enough." He contended that for this reason we should begin adult education.

Winston Churchill said, "Time may be short."

Mr. Luce, the editor of *Life, Time,* and *Fortune* magazines, addressed a group of missionaries who were the first to return to their fields after the war. Speaking in San Francisco, he made the statement that when he was a boy, the son of a Presbyterian missionary in China, he and his father often discussed the premillennial coming of Christ, and he thought that all missionaries who believed in that teaching were inclined to be fanatical. And then Mr. Luce said, "I wonder if there wasn't something to that position after all."

It is very interesting to note that *The Christian Century* carried an article by Wesner Fallaw (of all journals, this one seems to be the most unlikely in which to read a statement like this) which said, "A function of the Christian is to make preparation for world's end."

Dr. Charles Beard, the American historian, says, "All over the world the thinkers and searchers who scan the horizon of the future are attempting to assess the values of civilization and speculating about its destiny."

Dr. William Yogt, in the *Road to Civilization,* said, "The handwriting on the wall of five continents now tells us that the Day of Judgment is at hand."

Dr. Raymond B. Fosdick, President of the Rockefeller Foundation, said, "To many ears comes the sound of the tramp of doom. Time is short."

H. G. Wells declared before he died, "This world is at

the end of its tether. The end of everything we call life is close at hand."

General Douglas MacArthur said, "We have had our last chance."

Former President Dwight Eisenhower said, "Without a moral regeneration throughout the world there is no hope for us as we are going to disappear one day in the dust of an atomic explosion."

And Dr. Nicholas Murray Butler, ex-President of Columbia University, said, "The end cannot be far distant."

If men from all walks of life are speaking in this manner, certainly you and I, who have believed the Bible and who have had all these years such a clear statement concerning the judgment that is coming upon this world and the way in which it is to be destroyed, should be alert. Do not misunderstand me, I am not saying that the atomic bomb will be God's method for the destruction of this world. I am merely saying that man at last has found out that this passage in 2 Peter makes good sense. This is a way that is not only logical but is scientific by which God can destroy this universe.

Notwithstanding, this is something that should not alarm God's people, and the reason it should not alarm God's people is that we have a blessed hope.

The Believer's Blessed Hope

We are not looking for the atomic destruction of this world; we are looking for the Lord from heaven. I am confident that this is the next thing which is in God's program for His people—we shall have more to say concerning this in the next section. Certainly there is here a warning to the unsaved. If you are without Christ and are living without God in this world, certainly there is a message in this for you.

In verse 9 we read:

The Lord is not slow about his promise as some count slowness, but is forbearing toward you, not wishing that any should perish, but that all should reach repentance.

It is not God's will that you should perish. One of the reasons that you have read this message is simply because God does not want you to come into judgment, but He wants you to pass from death unto life.

And you can do that—you can turn to Him and receive the wonderful salvation that He has for you. It is His gift to you, for He says:

Verily, verily I say unto you, He that heareth my word, and believeth on him that sent me, hath everlasting life, and shall not come into condemnation; but is passed from death unto life. (John 5:24)

Did you know that you cannot keep God from loving you? You can reject His love, but you cannot keep Him from loving you. You cannot keep it from raining, but you can raise an umbrella to keep the rain from falling on you. At this moment God's love is falling around you—certainly showers of mercy are falling on this earth—and you can raise the umbrella of indifference, you can raise the umbrella of skepticism, you can raise the umbrella of your own self-will, but you cannot keep God from loving you.

There is a story that comes out of Greek mythology concerning a young man who had a very godly mother, but he fell in love with a very ungodly girl. The ungodly girl hated the boy's mother and could not bear to be in her presence. It was not because the mother rebuked her, but her very character and her very presence were a rebuke to this girl. Nevertheless, this boy was desperately in love with her, for she was beautiful. And finally he pleaded with her to marry him, and she said, "Only on one condition; you must cut out your mother's heart and bring it to me." Well, this boy was so madly in love and so desperate that he descended to the low plane of committing this diabolical deed. He killed his mother, cut out her heart and was taking it to the girl when, on the way, he stumbled and fell. The heart spoke out, "My son, did you hurt yourself?"

My friend, you can slap God in the face, you can turn your back on Him, you can blaspheme Him, but you cannot keep Him from wanting to save you. And He does want to save you, and He will save you if you will turn to Him and receive the salvation that He offers in Jesus Christ.

THE WORLD THAT WILL BE

Turning to the twenty-first chapter of the book of Revelation, I want you to notice this language.

And I saw a new heaven and a new earth: for the first heaven and the first earth were passed away; and there was no more sea. And I John saw the holy city, new Jerusalem, coming down from God out of heaven, prepared as a bride adorned for her husband. And I heard a great voice out of heaven saying, Behold, the tabernacle of God is with men, and he will dwell with them, and they shall be his people, and God himself shall be with them, and be their God. And God shall wipe away all tears from their eyes; and there shall be no more death, neither sorrow, nor crying, neither shall there be any more pain: for the former things are passed away. And he that sat upon the throne said, Behold, I make all things new. And he said unto me, Write: for these words are true and faithful. And he said unto me, It is done. I am Alpha and Omega, the beginning and the end. I will give unto him that is athirst of the fountain of the water of life freely. He that overcometh shall inherit all things; and I will be his God, and he shall be my son. But the fearful, and unbelieving, and the abominable, and murderers, and fornicators, and sorcerers, and idolaters, and all liars, shall have their part in the lake which burneth with fire and brimstone: which is the second death. (Revelation 21:1–8)

Now as we turn to the world that will be, it might be well for us to tie the strings of this message together. We first saw "The World That Was"—that world of the past; then "The World That Is"—this present world; and now "The World That Will Be" —the world of the future. Actually, these are three time periods of the world.

Concerning the world that was—it perished, perished in a judgment of water. The reference here in 2 Peter to that destruction can refer to the flood of Noah's day (there being ample evidence for that), but it can likewise refer to that period which may be between Genesis 1:1 and Genesis 1:2 in which the earth became without form and void. During that period, we find water covering the face of this earth and then God moving in, drawing the land out of the water. There may have been a pre-Adamic judgment, concerning which we know very little. We see only the scar marks, and the stones bear mute evidence to the fact that there was a judgment on the earth.

The second time period is "The World That Is." The world in which we are living is a world which is moving to judgment, not a judgment again by water, not a submerging or an immersing in water, but a judgment of fire. The language of Peter is striking, as we saw in the preceding section. He speaks of the elements; that is, the basic materials, these little rows of blocks, the atoms, being unloosed, being untied. What is known today as atomic fission may be the method God will use to unloose the atoms of this universe.

Do not misunderstand me, I do not know whether man has found out all of God's secrets or not. We do know this: Man has broken into God's treasure house where He has put these things in store, and man has found out God's secret, an awful secret, the method by which this universe *can* be destroyed some day, the method by which God may move in. And man has opened Pandora's box, turning loose upon this world a veritable plague, putting a fear in the heart of mankind. Men in all walks of life, not just preachers but informed men everywhere are dreading what the future holds. A judgment is coming upon this present world. God's Word speaks of that.

The best commentary to be found on 2 Peter 3 is the atomic bomb. Atomic fission has thrown more light on this chapter than has any commentary.

Now then we come to "The World That Will Be."

The Destruction of This Present World

Since this present world is to be destroyed, there are several problems which arise in the mind.

When will it be destroyed? I want to make a rather startling statement: I think we can know the time this is going to take place. Do not misunderstand me. I am not setting dates, and I do not believe we can know the dates. We can know only the chronological order of the events, which seems to me to be the important thing.

Men today visualize this universe of the future devoid of life, a satellite like the moon, with not a vestige of life, either plant or animal, on topside of it because of man's inhumanity to man.

May I just pause a moment to say this: Premillennialism is under attack today. (I am a premillennialist, and I trust you are.) Premillennialism is a system that presents God's program, but any man who sets a date for the events of this program removes himself from the realm of the sound teachers of the premillennial school.

Now let us go into the question as to when this present world will be destroyed. Please note carefully the language again, for we are after something else in these verses. Look again at 2 Peter 3:7.(RSV)

> *But by the same word the heavens and earth that now exist have been stored up for fire, being kept until the day of judgment and destruction of ungodly men.*

When does this destruction of ungodly men and the judgment of ungodly men take place? Well, beloved, it does not take place until after the Millennium. It does not take place until the Great White Throne judgment when, we are told, the dead are raised. To me, that is the most striking language one can find. The Word says that the unbelieving dead are to be raised. If they are raised, are they not alive? No, they are still dead; they are spiritually dead. But they are raised out of the grave to stand before a holy God—these people who thought it was not necessary to seek refuge from their sins in the blood of our Savior, who have been rejecting it down through the ages and have said that they will stand before God on their own merits and by their own works at the time of the judgment. This judgment takes place after the Millennium, when this present earth will be destroyed and when the new earth and the new heaven come into view.

How will the day of the Lord come? We have further means of answering that question in verse 10:

> **But the day of the Lord will come like a thief, and then the heavens will pass away with a loud noise, and the elements will be dissolved with fire.**

"The day of the Lord" is an expression with which all of us should be familiar. It is an Old Testament expression used by the first of the writing prophets and continuing down through the prophets. It refers to a time of judgment that is coming upon this earth; it refers to the beginning of that awful day known as the Great Tribulation, continuing even through the Millennium and all the way to the Great White Throne of Almighty God. All of this period is "the day of the Lord" because God is moving in to straighten out the affairs of this world.

In connection with the Great Tribulation period, I should like to remind you that this is one period through which you and I, as God's people, will not have to pass.

There is a time of great trouble coming upon this earth, and the world is moving into it just as a boat moves into a tornado or a typhoon at sea. But God's people are promised that they are going to be delivered from that time of trouble.

We are not looking for the Lord to come as a thief. You know that when you are looking for a thief, you barricade the door, putting extra locks on it to try to shut him out. But, my beloved, for the believer the coming of Christ is a blessed hope. It is something against which the believer does not lock his door—he opens the door and welcomes the day of His coming. But He will come as a thief in the night to an unbelieving world that wants to shut Him out and would shut Him out if it were possible.

We are also looking for a new heaven and a new earth. Will you listen to this language:

> *But according to his promise we wait for new heavens and a new earth in which righteousness dwells. Therefore, beloved, since you wait for these, be zealous to be found by him without spot or blemish, and at peace.* (2 Peter 3:13–14)

You and I are looking, not for the Great Tribulation to come or a time of trouble or worldwide nuclear devastation, but for the Lord from heaven. That is still the blessed hope of the church. By the way, keep in mind that all through the Bible the word *church* refers to the whole body of true believers.

The Believer and the Tribulation

We are told repeatedly in the Word of God that God's people are to be delivered from the Great Tribulation. I should like to turn to two or three passages to show you how clear the Bible is on this. In Romans 2:5 we read language like the following:

*But after thy hardness and impenitent heart treasurest
up unto thyself wrath against the day of wrath and revelation of the righteous judgment of God.*

Paul here is talking about the judgment that is coming and
the day of wrath that is coming upon ungodly men who
reject Christ. But notice what he said to those who trusted
Christ in Romans 5:9:

*Much more then, being now justified by his blood, we
shall be saved from wrath through him.*

The blood of Christ, my beloved, is the reason His church
is not going through the Tribulation. It is because He paid
the price, delivering His church from that awful day. In 1
Thessalonians 1:10 we read of the hope which is given to
the church:

*And to wait for his Son from heaven, whom he raised
from the dead, even Jesus, who delivered us from the
wrath to come.*

He has delivered His church from the wrath to come, but
that day is coming. In 1 Thessalonians 5:9 we read:

*For God hath not appointed us to wrath but to obtain
salvation by our Lord Jesus Christ.*

Why the Believer Does Not Go Through the Tribulation

The Grace of God Would Be Frustrated. If you should ask
me for the main reason why the church will not go through
the Great Tribulation, I would say to you that for the
church to go through the Tribulation would frustrate the
grace of God. There are people who say, "If you trust
Christ, He will save you; but, of course, you will have to go
through the Tribulation, a time of awful trouble here upon
this earth." But that is to frustrate the grace of God! If you
are saved by grace, you have been saved from all judgment

and all wrath, and the grace of God that saves you from sin is the same grace of God that can deliver you from this time of wrath that is coming upon the earth.

The Church Would Have No Intercessor. The second reason the church will not go through the Tribulation is that during the Tribulation period Christ leaves the throne of intercession and becomes the Judge. If the church were still on the earth, this would mean that the church had no Intercessor in heaven. The very minute that the Lord moves from the place of intercession, He has in that minute taken the church to be with Him. The reason that the Lord is in heaven at the right hand of God this very moment is to make intercession for those who are His own.

The Tribulation Saints Pray for Revenge. The Tribulation saints, those who trust Christ during that awful period, pray for revenge, and their prayer is answered. But the church is never asked to pray for revenge. We are told definitely *not* to pray for revenge, but rather to leave that in the hands of God and to pray for those who despitefully use us.

If the church were to go through the Great Tribulation, the edge of the blessed hope would be dulled. But we do not go through that awful time; we are looking for the Lord from heaven—that is the great pulsating hope for the church.

Order of Events

This time of great trouble which is coming upon the earth is spoken of in the Word of God as being unparalleled in the history of the world. The Lord Jesus called it the Great Tribulation. He said there had been nothing like it before and there would be nothing like it afterward. That is the reason I know we are not now in the Tribulation—we are not in a period of trouble that we could not match somewhere else in history. When the world gets into the time of the Great Tribulation, nobody will ask, "Are we in it?" Brother, they will know it!

After that, the Millennium takes place, which is the

thousand years' reign of Christ over the earth. Immediately following the Millennium, the devil is released for a little season—the reason I do not know. Someone once went to Dr. Chafer, saying, "Dr. Chafer, after God puts the devil down in the bottomless pit, why in the world would He turn him loose again?" Dr. Chafer said in reply, "Well, that is a problem, but if you will tell me why God turned the devil loose in the first place, I will tell you why God will turn him loose in the second place."

God is going to turn him loose again for a little while, and at that time he will gather together all those who are in rebellion against God. Then the judgment comes, the Great White Throne judgment, after which the new heaven and the new earth come into view, because this earth and the present heaven are to be destroyed.

The New Heaven and the New Earth

Now let us turn to Revelation 21 which we quoted at the beginning of this section, and we shall look for some very specific things concerning the new heaven and the new earth. However, our first reference is in 2 Peter 3, verse 13:

"Righteousness dwells." It is interesting, is it not, that in the world that was, righteousness was a possibility? In this present world righteousness is provided for those who trust Christ. In the millennial world righteousness will cover the earth as the waters cover the sea. But in the new earth that is to appear, righteousness will be at home. It will dwell. It will never leave. To be in a world where everything is right will be wonderful!

This earth is not the dwelling place of righteousness now, in spite of what a great many people are saying. The fact of the matter is there is nothing right in this world. Shakespeare put it, "The times are out of joint." Browning was wrong in his "Pippa Passes" when he made the statement, "The lark's on the wing, the snail's on the thorn, God's in His heaven and all is right with the world." God is in His heaven, but all is not right with this world. In fact, everything is all wrong.

But there is coming a new earth in which everything is going to be right. The righteousness of God will have its abode there as it never has in the past. Now you talk about a platform for a new order for the Democrats or for the Republicans or for the Communists. I want to give you the platform for this new earth—mere man cannot match what God has in mind for this earth. The first thing that is going to be true is that God will be here:

> *He will dwell with them, and they shall be his people, and God himself shall be with them, and be their God.* (Revelation 21:3)

That is going to be a glorious day! Although God is here now through the Holy Spirit, and Jesus Christ would like to make Himself real to you, He is not dwelling on this earth now. God is *going* to dwell on this earth. What a program—what a glorious program that will be!

"God shall wipe away all tears from their eyes" (Revelation 21:4). Is that not a wonderful platform? He is going to wipe away all tears. Think of the heartache today in this world. Think of the broken hearts and the frustrated lives on topside of this earth. Things are not right down here, but some day God is going to make them right. He is going to wipe away all tears. What a glorious and wonderful day that is going to be yonder in the future!

"There shall be no more death" (Revelation 21:4). Death is the last enemy that is going to be put down. Death is going to occur in the Millennium—there will be people who will die during the Millennium because the last enemy to be destroyed will be death; but in this new earth, death will not be present. Thank God for that! Death is the great enemy of mankind; death is *your* great enemy. My friend, death is stalking you, and one of these days, if the Lord tarries, he will get you. Death is moving up and down this

earth. He is the one that is getting the victory—he is the one that got the victory over Hitler, he is the one who got the victory over Mussolini and Joe Stalin. Death will stop every man one of these days. Death is the great enemy of all mankind. But, thank God, there is a day coming when we will not have to go to the cemetery any more. The day is coming when we will never have to put a loved one in the grave. In the new earth, death is to be removed.

"Neither shall there be any more pain" (Revelation 21:4). Think of the suffering that is on the topside of this earth. In the new earth which is coming some day, there will be no pain, no more hospitals, no more suffering.

"I make all things new" (Revelation 21:5). We have been stressing the fact that the earth which comes into being after the present one is destroyed is to be new, and here we are told that all things will be made new. I would like to refer you also in this connection to Isaiah 65:17:

> *. . . Behold, I create new heavens and a new earth, and the former shall not be remembered, nor come into mind.*

This new earth is going to be so wonderful that we are going to forget all about this earth on which we now live. Some of us have had the experience of looking at the new automobiles, and when we look at a new model and then get back into our old car, it looks worse than we had thought. It is very discouraging to drive off with the old paint job, the same old jalopy, after looking at the new models. Someday there will be a new earth. God has this new model earth which will be coming into view. The thing that characterizes it is newness. I know nothing about it, but I have done a great deal of speculating. I think there will be so many changes that we will not recognize the new earth when we see it in that day.

There will be no evil there:

*But the fearful, and unbelieving, and the abominable,
and murderers, and fornicators [sexually immoral],
and sorcerers, and idolaters, and all liars, shall have
their part in the lake which burneth with fire and brimstone.* (Revelation 21:8)

There is a very definite reason for it. We find it revealed in
the record of Lot and his wife fleeing Sodom. When she
left that city of Sodom, she left all of her interests there.
She loved "Lot," but it was a *lot* of Sodom that she loved.
She had her heart wrapped up in the things of Sodom. I
think she belonged to the bridge clubs; she belonged to the
Shakespeare club; she belonged to all the important clubs
in the city of Sodom. She was in society. Her sons and
daughters had married into Sodomite society—in fact, they
had married Sodomites. Awful thing! And she lost most of
her children—she left all of them back there but two. When
she left the city, she turned around and looked back. Do
you know why she looked back? Because she did not believe God would destroy the city. There are a lot of people
today who do not think that there is a judgment coming
upon this world. Mrs. Lot did not believe it either. She
could not imagine that the wonderful culture of Sodom
was so God-dishonoring that a holy God was going to destroy it. And so she turned and looked back.

I wish we had a picture of her when she looked back. I
think you would have seen tragic longing in the face of that
woman. Her children were back there and that is where her
interests were. And I will tell you, she died when she
moved out of Sodom—her heart turned to stone and her
body to salt.

My friend, how do you feel toward this world? You do
not have to withdraw to a monastery. You do not have to
build a fence around yourself. The Lord Jesus said to the
Father, "I pray that you keep them in the world." He
wants to keep us in the world down here, but He doesn't
want the world in us. It ought to lead us to holy living as we

see these things happening around us today and read of events that are coming to pass.

And then there is something else I would like to say. These things ought to have an effect on those who are without God and without hope in this world. It ought to make them very solemn and very serious. Perhaps in the past you have ridiculed this Bible and you have disbelieved its prophetic warnings and you have not enjoyed reading about the hour of doom that is coming upon this earth. But, my friend, men from all walks of life—editors, educators, scientists, statesmen—look out at this world and view the future with alarm. Winston Churchill called it "the awful unfolding scene of the future." Dr. Adolph Keller, probably the best-informed man in Europe as far as the church is concerned, said, "We don't understand in Europe what you people are talking about when you speak of building a new order. We know in Europe that an old order has come to its death. It is dying; it is on the way out." And then he made this statement: "It's five minutes to twelve in the history of the world."

Judgment for the Unbeliever

My beloved, if men from all walks of life are talking in this manner, what should be the attitude of an unbeliever who has turned his back upon God? In view of the fact that we are moving into impending judgment, what should be your attitude? Do not let the patience of God deceive you. Hear Him again.

> *The Lord is not slow about his promise, as some count slowness; but is forbearing toward you, not wishing that any should perish, but that all should reach repentance.* (2 Peter 3:9)

God is very patient. God has plenty of time. Do you know the reason He is not moving forward today? It is because He has eternity behind Him and eternity ahead of Him. He

is not crowded for time—He is not rushing to catch a train
—He is not rushing to keep an appointment at a certain
time. God has eternity, and He is in no hurry. And then
again, He is very patient. And the patience of God deceives
many. An Old Testament writer said it like this:

> *Because judgment against an evil work is not executed
> speedily, the heart of the sons of men is fully set in them
> to do evil.* (Ecclesiastes 8:11)

Because God does not move immediately, do not be
deceived. He is going to move in time, and that is His
message for this present hour.

You remember that when Paul went into that decadent
city of Athens which was then living on past glory, the
glory that had been Greece, the Athenians were skeptical
and cynical as they listened to the gospel. And Paul told
them there:

> *The times of this ignorance God overlooked; but now
> commandeth all men everywhere to repent.* (Acts 17:30)

That is His message today, my friend, because of His impending judgment.

And when Paul went in to talk with Felix, he reasoned
with that man concerning righteousness and temperance
and judgment to come. That is part of the program of
God. You may feel that I am old-fashioned myself, that I
am outmoded and a back number to be talking about these
things, but this is the Word of God. God is patient and it is
not His will that any should perish but that all should come
to know Him.

In a southern city a very prominent judge was out for
lunch. As he started to cross the street, he saw a young
man step in the pathway of an oncoming truck. This judge
made a leap and grabbed the young man, throwing him out
of the pathway of that truck. When he took him out of the

way, the people around heaved sighs of relief, and the young man thanked him profusely. The judge went on his way. Weeks passed and even months went by. Then this young man was arrested for a very serious crime. He was brought into the court of this judge. When he came into the presence of the judge, he recognized him and was just waiting for his opportunity to speak. When that time came, he said to the judge, "You know me, Judge. You know me."

The judge replied, "Young man, I don't think I do."

He said, "Yes, you know me. Don't you remember? One day at the corner of (and he identified the spot) you rescued a young man. Well, I was the young man. Can't you help me today?"

The judge looked down at this young man who had committed the awful crime, and there was silence in the courtroom. Finally, the judge said, "Young man, the other day I was your savior. Today I am your judge."

Today the Lord Jesus Christ is your Savior. Tomorrow He will be your Judge.

May I close with this little story? Dr. Harry Rimmer told it. It concerns the water supply of Los Angeles. They tell me that it costs $25,000,000 to turn on a spigot in order to get a drop of water here. There was a dam built over here in the mountains not far from us without proper tests being made. The dam was anchored to the rock on the side, but it was the kind of rock that crumbled when it was saturated with water. After the dam was filled, as time went on, it began to give way without being detected. One night the night watchman in making his rounds came off the dam and was just coming into the powerhouse when he heard an awful, awful crash. He turned to see the dam going out and a great wall of water rushing down. He knew that below were multitudes of people who would be destroyed. He rushed to the telephone and called one town after another, warning them that the destruction was on the way. When the word was brought to a little town down in the pathway of the water, the sheriff there went out and there in the very bed of this river was camped a group of Mexicans. They were there to pick fruit and had a regular little tent town. They laughed and refused to believe that a flood could come. They looked at the moon and said, "How could there be a flood? The moon is shining." The sheriff continued to warn them, but they refused to listen. Finally he had to move on to warn others. It is said that many of their bodies were washed two and three miles out to sea when the deluge came to their little tent town.

And multitudes at this moment are looking around them saying, "The moon is shining" or "the sun is still shining. The deluge is not coming." My friend, it is coming. Today He is your Savior. Tomorrow He will be your Judge.

13

WHAT CAN BELIEVERS DO IN DAYS OF APOSTASY?

(The Epistle of Jude)

Beloved, when I gave all diligence to write unto you of the common salvation, it was needful for me to write unto you, and exhort you that ye should earnestly contend for the faith which was once delivered unto the saints. For there are certain men crept in unawares, who were before of old ordained to this condemnation, ungodly men, turning the grace of our God into lasciviousness, and denying the only Lord God, and our Lord Jesus Christ. . . . But, beloved, remember ye the words which were spoken before by the apostles of our Lord Jesus Christ; how that they told you there should be mockers in the last time, who should walk after their own ungodly lusts. These are they who separate themselves, sensual, having not the Spirit. But ye, beloved, building up yourselves on your most holy faith, praying in the Holy Spirit, keep yourselves in the love of God, looking for the mercy of our Lord Jesus Christ unto eternal life. And of some have compassion, making a difference; and others save with fear, pulling

them out of the fire, hating even the garment spotted by the flesh. (Jude 3–4, 17–23)★

Many of us who have been preaching that someday there would be an apostasy in the church never believed we would live to see what has happened in our day or how far along the organized church now is in apostasy. In the epistle of Jude this man, a half-brother of the Lord Jesus, wrote intending as he tells us to write on one of the common doctrines of the church. He could have written about many things, or about any one of many, but the Spirit of God deterred him and detoured him and caused him to write on the apostasy. That gives, then, a note of alarm to the epistle. The Spirit of God felt this was such an important subject that it was necessary to turn Jude from writing on what he intended and to write instead on this particular subject.

WHAT DO YOU MEAN, APOSTASY?

The word *apostasy* means to stand away from the truth. It comes from two Greek words, *apo histemi. Apo* is a little preposition which means "away from," and *histemi* means "to stand." Apostasy can only take place in a church or in a so-called believer who professes to believe something and then moves away from it—he stands away from it and no longer holds what he professed to believe at one time.

Webster, who always does a good job of defining words, says that the apostasy is the "abandonment of what one has voluntarily professed; total desertion of the principles of faith." Abandonment of that which was voluntarily professed—our Lord used that expression when He was giving

---

★ All Scripture references from *The New Scofield Reference Bible*.

the parable of the sower. Referring to the seed that fell on the rock, He said:

> *They on the rock are they who, when they hear, receive the word with joy; and these have no root, who for a while believe, and in time of testing fall away.* (Luke 8:13)

"Fall away" is the Greek *aphistemi*—they apostatize. They professed to believe, then they moved away from it. They no longer believe. They have departed from the faith.

Apostasy would be impossible among unevangelized tribes who had never heard the gospel. An apostate is one who has not only heard the gospel but has professed to believe the gospel, and then departs from it. That's apostasy.

This word occurs also in Hebrews:

> *Take heed, brethren, lest there be in any of you an evil heart of unbelief, in departing from the living God.* (Hebrews 3:12)

Here are those who have professed to believe. Now they no longer believe. They have departed from it.

Time and again I have heard this among preachers. There are today thousands of men in the ministry (and they're an unhappy lot) who can say, "I once professed it, but I no longer believe it."

It may surprise you to know that Karl Marx was an apostate. This is the man who wrote *Das Kapital,* the basis of communism and world revolution. He was brought up in a Christian home. His father, who descended from a long line of rabbis, accepted Christian baptism for himself and his family when Karl was six years old. Young Karl attended the gymnasium at Trier, and his examination papers from when he left school have been discovered. The one that gained the most unqualified approval was a theo-

logical essay on "the union of the faithful in Christ according to John 15:1–14, portrayed in its origin and essence, in
its unconditional necessity and in its effect." That is quite
a subject for a young fellow! It was marked by the teacher
as a thoughtful, copious, and powerful presentation of the
theme. The boy was seventeen when he wrote this essay in
1835. This is the man who went on to write the ideology
for godless states. He was an apostate. He once professed
to believe something. There came a day when he stood
away from it; he no longer believed it.

All the New Testament writers speak of the approaching
apostasy. To them it was just a little cloud on the horizon,
the size of a man's hand. But that cloud has now darkened
and covered the sky. Today you and I are in the storm. We
are seeing one of the greatest departures from the faith in
the history of the church.

Jude is the book in the New Testament that deals almost
exclusively with the apostasy. Jude begins his subject with
verse 4:

> *For there are certain men crept in unawares, who were
> before of old ordained to this condemnation.* . . .

He warns against these certain men who have crept in unawares. "Ordained" here means they were written of beforehand. This is not something new, Jude says. They
"were long beforehand marked out for this condemnation." We went through a period when some theologians
said that God was dead. Of course they would say that
because they were "ungodly men," and God was not even
in their thinking.

> . . . *Turning the grace of our God into lasciviousness,
> and denying the only Lord God, and our Lord Jesus
> Christ.* (Jude 4)

A better understood translation would be, "They turned
the grace of our God into blatant immorality." You see, the

difference today is the fact that sin, which before was carried on under cover (I'm perfectly willing to admit that there was sin and unbelief in the church before) is today blatant. Immorality has come out in the open. Ministers in our great denominations are saying that adultery, lying, and stealing are perfectly permissible. They have turned the grace of our God into blatant immorality.

Some years ago in Washington, D.C., a minister said, "We liberal churchmen are no longer interested in the fundamental-modernist controversy. We do not believe we should even waste our time engaging in it. So far as we are concerned, it makes no difference whether Christ was born of a virgin or not. We don't even bother to form an opinion on the subject."

An Arlington, Virginia, minister said, "We have closed our minds to such trivial considerations as the question of the resurrection of Christ. If you fundamentalists wish to believe that nonsense, we have no objection, but we have more important things to preach than the presence or absence of an empty tomb twenty centuries ago."

A leading minister in Washington, D.C., said flatly, "In our denomination what you call 'the faith of our fathers' is approaching total extinction. Of course a few of the older ministers still cling to the Bible, but among the younger men, the real leaders of our denomination today, I do not know a single one who believes in Christ or any of the things that you classify as fundamentals."

Another man said,

We are interested in human life and human destiny on earth. We don't know or care whether there is a life beyond the grave. We presume there is a God, but we know that He will ever be a mystery to us. We do not know or care whether God possesses personality or not. He may be just an impersonal force. Religion means very little, if anything. In the modern world religion has no vital place. The function of the modern minister is to guide the thinking people along social and economic lines. Morals, like religion, are out of date. The world today requires a new social order. The younger generation won't need either morals or religion if we create a social order without ignorance or poverty. We are moving in the direction of the elimination of prayer from our services entirely. We still include it occasionally to please those who are accustomed to it, for prayer is a sort of habit with folks. It takes time to educate them to a realization that it is a hangover from the religious past. We do not teach Bible to our young people. We do not teach them to pray. Our youth program is centered around recreation.

Friend, at the present moment and for some time now the church has been engaged in a great brainwashing program to absolutely get rid of the Word of God. Now, I went to school with some of these fellows, and I know what kind of grades they made, so that their intellectual facade is interesting indeed. It is my feeling that real believers ought to wake up at this hour.

You see, the apostasy is not outside the church. It is on the inside. The severest attack upon the Word of God, upon the Christian faith, and upon the church is coming from inside the church. So much so that when the American Association for the Advancement of Atheism disbanded their organization a number of years ago, Smith, who headed it, gave this as his reason, "The pulpit is doing a much better job than we are doing!" He felt that the work of the atheists' association was no longer needed. You no longer see the greatest attack upon the Word of God made in the city square where the soapbox orators hold forth— they are pikers. Go to some liberal church today and you will hear the greatest attack upon the Word of God. The Bible is being discredited all across America every Sunday morning.

It was Horatius Bonar, a great saint of the past, who made this statement in light of the little epistle of Jude, "In some ages evil seems to sleep. In the last days it will awake to full life and activity. It will seize every instrument: the press, the pulpit, the platform." Today evil has taken over the press; it has taken over the pulpit and the platform.

Bonar continues: "It will enlist every science and art—music, sculpture, painting, portrait, philosophy—making them all subservient to its development. The multiplication of crimes, contempt of laws, blasphemies—these are the specimens of the energy of evil." In this day in which you and I live these are the things that fill our morning newspaper. There is no use for me to recount *ad nauseum* the things that are happening in our contemporary society. We are now in the midst of the apostasy.

Way back in the days of Bernard of Cluny, that wonderful saint of God (and he was that), he said,

> *The days are very evil,*
> *   the times are waxing late;*
> *Be sober and keep vigil—*
> *   the Judge is at the gate.*
>
> *The Judge who comes in mercy*
> *   the Judge who comes with might,*
> *To terminate the evil*
> *   and diadem the right.*

WHAT CAN WE DO TODAY?

Now these are the days in which we are living, and the question is, what can believers do in days of apostasy and revolution? What can we do today? Well, Jude answers this question in his epistle, and it is not a negative answer. He tells us that there are seven things that believers can do in days like these in which we are living. Up to this point he has described the apostasy, and believe me, he paints a dark picture. But now he is speaking to believers: "But ye, beloved," do these things:

1. *"Building up yourselves on your most holy faith"* (verse 20). The word "faith" is actually *the* faith, the body of truth that has been given to us in the Bible. All the way through the Word of God there is that constant injunction upon believers to get into the Word of God. This today is our shelter; this is our armor; this is our protection; this is our help. And we're told again and again, "grow in grace"; "study to show thyself approved unto God"; "give attendance to reading"; "meditate upon these things"!

When the first church came into existence, it is said that they "continued steadfastly in the apostles' doctrine" (Acts 2:42), which was *the* faith, that body of truth that has come down to us in the Word of God. We must build up ourselves in that if we are to stand.

In other words, we are to study the Word of God. Since God gave sixty-six books, He meant that we are to study all sixty-six of them—not only the three or four that are our favorites. How many Bible classes go back and forth, teaching John, Romans, and probably they'll teach Revelation—but what about the other sixty-three books that are in the Bible? Why don't we study them? Why don't we study *all* of them?

My friend, if you are going to build yourself up in your most holy faith, you must have the total Word of God. You can't build a house without a foundation. And when you get the foundation laid, you will need to put up some timbers to hold the roof. And you will need a roof on it. You will need sides on it. You will want to fix it up on the inside. And you need all sixty-six books of the Bible if you are going to build up yourself on your most holy faith.

Paul urges us to study the Word of God. He said,

> *Study to show thyself approved unto God, a workman that needeth not to be ashamed, rightly dividing the word of truth.* (2 Timothy 2:15)

We are to *study!* And he added:

> *All scripture is given by inspiration of God, and is profitable for doctrine, for reproof, for correction, for instruction in righteousness.* (2 Timothy 3:16)

In other words, the recourse that you and I have in these days is the Word of God.

Now the reason many fall by the wayside is that the Seed has fallen among stones. It didn't get deeply rooted. The Word of God is the Seed, and unless you study all the the Bible, getting down in the good rich soil, you are not going to become a very healthy looking plant. And it won't be long until you are trampled down and burned out by the sun.

Peter in his second epistle says,

> *We have also a more sure word of prophecy, unto which ye do well that ye take heed, as unto a light that shineth in a dark place, until the day dawn, and the day star arise in your hearts; knowing this first, that no prophecy of the scripture is of any private interpretation.* (2 Peter 1:19–20)

Don't pull out just one or two verses and think you have it, my friend. That is the tragedy of Bible study today—drawing out a few verses here and a few verses there and building a system. Why not take it all? Certainly there are parts of the Word of God that you are not going to like. It steps on your toes, or it runs counter to current philosophy, but it is necessary to build up ourselves on our most holy faith.

In other words, when you get into days of apostasy, the compass and the chart that you have is the Word of God. This is the reason I have built my ministry entirely upon the Word of God. I believe it is our only hope.

Now as to these pastors who say they do not believe nor teach the Bible, I am wondering how many people are interested in their liberal message today. In spite of days of apostasy, I find that there is a great heart-hunger on the part of many folk. They want a sure word from God Himself in this hour of uncertainty. They want to know what *He* says.

At the turn of the century there was a movement in the

church away from preaching and teaching the Bible. I remember as a boy going to church how ignorant I was—I knew nothing, and I knew nothing even after I'd been to church because the Word of God was never preached. It was always a service built on emotion. Or it was a book review. Or it had to do with some sort of entertainment. As a result, we have in America a "Christian" civilization of the most biblically illiterate people who ever have been on topside of the earth. The common man in Germany after the Reformation knew more about the Word of God than does the average man in America today.

The tragedy is that even believers are ignorant of the Bible. In this hour of apostasy God's people need not only to say they believe in the Word of God from cover to cover, but they need to know what is between the covers. In this day of confusion and compromise you need to build up yourself in the most holy faith by a serious study of the Word of God.

Let me remind you that the Bible is unique. It is a Book that is different from any other book. It is written by men and they include in it their own personalities—God did not disturb that at all. But He so guided them that when they had finished, God had gotten through His message to man without error.

Not only is it without error, but this Book still has power. Paul writes to the Thessalonians:

> *For our gospel came not unto you in word only, but also in power, and in the Holy Spirit, and in much assurance, as ye know what manner of men we were among you for your sake.* (1 Thessalonians 1:5)

This Book has a message for those who will hear it, a message that will transform hearts and lives. The Word of God is not only a chart and compass, but it is our powerhouse. My friend, you cannot be ignorant of the Word of God and live the Christian life!

2. ***"Praying in the Holy Spirit"*** (verse 20) is the second thing Jude says we can do in days of apostasy. And that's a particular kind of prayer. Paul says in Ephesians 6:18, "Praying always with all prayer and supplication in the Spirit." Twice in the Scripture we are told to do that. And praying in the Holy Spirit is not turning in a grocery list to the Lord every morning or evening. It's really getting down and, in the Spirit, laying your heart bare before Him. And I believe we can talk to Him as we can talk to no one else.

Because I drive while alone quite a bit, I've been practicing something for the past few years. When I drove over to Phoenix recently, it took me six hours, and I had a wonderful time of it. Do you know why? The Lord Jesus sat with me. You say, "How do I know?" Because I talked to Him all the way over! I told Him what was on my heart. And I told Him about a lot of people—I told Him about the people I like, and I told Him about the people I don't like. He already knows how I feel—no use trying to keep anything from Him or trying to cover up.

You can tell Him how you feel! And I believe that is praying in the Holy Spirit today—when the Spirit of God leads us to Him where we can exhalt Him, we can praise Him and confess to Him and tell Him everything. How wonderful it is! We'd better start doing that in days of apostasy, because otherwise we may fall by the wayside—*you* can. We all can.

Paul, in writing to the Ephesians, chapter 6, verses 11 to 18, told them to "put on the whole armor of God," and you'll notice that every piece of that armor is for defense with the exception of two. Finally he speaks to them of "the sword of the Spirit, which is the *Word of God.*" We have no other offense than that except for "praying always with all prayer and supplication in the Spirit." This is the type of prayer that touches the throne of God. It is the type of prayer that gets things from God!

It was my theory, up until the time I was pastor of the Church of the Open Door in Los Angeles, that what we needed to do was to multiply numbers in a prayer meeting. I do not hold that view any longer. If you have ten people attending a prayer meeting and they are more or less spiritually asleep, it is not a very effective prayer meeting, I can tell you. But to multiply that number from ten to one hundred hasn't helped if you've brought in ninety more spiritually dull people. All you have now is a hundred dead people instead of ten dead people, and that has not helped the prayer meeting.

However, we do need those who will pray in the Holy Spirit. We need prayer that reaches through and touches the heart of God—prayer to which He *listens*.

I love that prayer in the ninth chapter of Daniel. Notice how he prepared himself:

> *And I set my face unto the Lord God, to seek by prayer and supplications, with fasting, and sackcloth, and ashes; and I prayed unto the LORD, my God, and made my confession.* . . . (Daniel 9:3–4)

And God dispatched an angel with an answer to his prayer. I think God said, "You go down and answer his prayer, but I'm going to keep listening to him." Daniel went on praying, and he touched the very heart of God.

Have you ever read any of Martin Luther's prayers? Oh, I tell you, when that man prayed, it was like storming the battlements of heaven! We hear very little praying like that today. But that is the type of prayer that absolutely transformed Europe—prayer in the Holy Spirit.

There are many times when we don't know what to pray for. I'll be honest with you—in my lifetime I have encountered problems that I have no solution for. I used to be able to give the Lord the best advice He ever had received on just how He ought to handle the thing. But I've learned that instead of going to Him with a program all outlined and saying, "Look here, Lord, this is the course You should follow," now I am more inclined to say, "Lord, I don't know the answer, but You do; if we get the right answer, it will have to come from You." Therefore—and I say it reverently—we can throw this back into the lap of God. And that's the way He wants it!

Years ago a missionary in Venezuela sent me a little card on which was a definition of prayer: "Prayer is the Holy Spirit, speaking in the believer, through Christ, to the Father." Friend, that is a very good definition of prayer.

Praying in the Holy Spirit means the Spirit of God leads and guides us in our prayer life. A great many folk say, "I pray for a certain thing and I don't get an answer." That ought to tell you something—you are not praying in the will of God! My grandson, when he was small, used to ask for more things that he shouldn't have than any little fellow I've ever met! I'd take him with me to the store sometimes, and he'd want everything he shouldn't have. I'd think to myself, *My, that's the way I pray!* Just like a little child, I say, "Lord, give me this and give me that," and He doesn't do it. Why? Because I am not praying in the Holy Spirit. Oh, to cast ourselves upon Him in days like these! In times of apostasy how we need to pray in the Holy Spirit.

3. *"Keep yourselves in the love of God"* (verse 21). Notice this exact language. Jude did not say that we are to do something to *win* the love of God. You are already *in* the love of God. Just keep yourself there. And friend, you cannot do anything to merit the love of God, neither can you keep Him from loving you.

Do you remember the rich young ruler who came to Jesus with a question? He wanted to know what he should do to inherit eternal life. And the record tells us:

> *Then Jesus, beholding him, loved him, and said unto him, One thing thou lackest; go thy way, sell whatever thou hast, and give to the poor, and thou shalt have treasure in heaven; and come, take up the cross, and follow me. And he was sad at that saying, and went*

away grieved; for he had great possessions. (Mark
10:21–22)

He turned and walked away from Christ, but the Lord still
loved him!

We need to recognize that God loves the believer. All
through the epistle of Jude he calls believers "beloved."
That doesn't mean that Jude loves them or that they love
him. It simply means they are beloved of *God*.

You see, you can't keep God from loving you. You can,
however, step out of the will of God so that you do not *feel*
the warmth of God's love in your life. So Jude says in effect, "Keep yourselves out there in the sunshine of His
love. Let His love flood your heart and flood your life."

It is the Spirit of God who makes the love of God real to
the believer. And that love of God is not our love for Him
but His love for us. The Holy Spirit makes it real to us.

I'm of the opinion that there are believers who are in
trouble today, many in a tough place, like the mother in
Dallas who had cancer and wanted to talk with me since I
myself was battling it. I told her, "You're talking to the
wrong one if you're looking for courage. I'm a coward. I'm
very frank to tell you, I wake up sometimes at two o'clock
in the morning in a cold sweat."

She said, "Dr. McGee, I have a boy and I have a girl,
and I've lost them. And my doctor tells me that I'll die
unless my nerves can become quieted again. I've been to
psychologists and psychiatrists. They can't help me. What
shall I do?"

So I asked her, "Do you believe God loves you?"

"I'm not sure of that."

"Well, He does love you. And if you're not sure of it, ask
Him to make it real to you. I had to do that. He made it
real to me and He'll make it real to you. But," I told her,
"whether you have that assurance or not, the Word of God
says that He loves you. He loved you when you were a
sinner, and since He loved you then and saved you, oh, He

loves you now! These problems you have, you can take them to Him and know that since He loves you He's going to give you the solution." Then I added, "But make sure you stay in His love."

She asked, "What do you mean?"

I said, "You know, you can't keep the sun from shining, but you can sure put up an umbrella and keep it off you. You can't keep it from raining here in Texas, but you can come in out of the rain and stay dry. There are a lot of folk today, a lot of Christians, who have put up an umbrella— an umbrella of indifference, an umbrella of sin, an umbrella of stepping out of the will of God—and they don't experience the love of God. But if you are willing to step into that circle of the will of God, if you're willing to confess the sins in your life, if you're willing to take down the umbrella and step out into the sunshine, you'll feel the warmth of His love."

A lot of folk need that today, because a great many of God's people are going through deep water. Recently I have been talking to a family that has been called upon to bear more than its share of trouble. It is a Christian family. The father (candidly, I wondered if he would make it or not) said to me the other day, "If it were not for the fact that I am persuaded that the Lord Jesus loves me, I'd give up the whole thing and walk out." But he won't be walking out because he has kept himself in the love of God.

How you and I need to keep ourselves in the light and warmth of God's love in these days!

4. *"Looking for the mercy of our Lord Jesus Christ unto eternal life"* (verse 21). The *mercy* of God is God's concern and care for you. Because of His mercy He was able to save you—He was concerned about you. He is rich in mercy. He has plenty of it. And we need all we can get because it is by mercy that God would even put up with us.

"Looking for the mercy of our Lord Jesus Christ" refers, I believe, to the coming of Christ for His church, the event we know as the Rapture of the church. You see, the reason I believe the church is not going through the Great Tribulation is that we are told to look for mercy, not judgment. I am not looking for judgment or the Great Tribulation. I am looking for the mercy of God.

A long time ago when He saved me, He did it by His mercy. And the very fact that He keeps holding on to me is an evidence of His mercy. If you meet me a million years from today in eternity and you find I'm still in heaven (and I will be there), I tell you now what I'll tell you then: I've been here a million years because He is merciful to me.

I am looking for the mercy of our Lord Jesus Christ. In days of apostasy we need to look for that, my beloved. In this day of failure, in this day of compromise, in this day of discouragement, we are to look for the mercy of our Lord Jesus Christ unto eternal life.

5. *"And of some have compassion, making a difference"* (verse 22). The better translation is, "And of some have compassion, who are in doubt." There are a great many good, sincere people today who do have their doubts, and we need to be patient with them.

In our Thursday night Bible study some years ago a woman came to me after every service for, I suppose, six weeks with one question after another. I began to have a feeling that she was trying to trap me or trick me and, frankly, I became a little impatient with her. Another lady was there with her, one of our church members. So one night I answered this woman's question rather sharply, and she turned and walked out. And the lady with her came to me and said, "Dr. McGee, just be patient with her. She is a very brilliant woman—she's in *Who's Who,* and she's been in practically every cult here in Southern California. She is really mixed up. And when you talk about 'Christ dying and paying the penalty for your sins,' and 'you just trust Him'—that's a new world to her, so give her time." So after that I would really answer her questions the best I could. About three months later she accepted Christ as her Savior. And I had a wonderful letter from her when she was back in Ohio, telling me of how the Lord was leading her.

There are some for whom we need to exercise compassion because they are in doubt, but they are honest. We are living in days when there is so much doubt cast upon the Word of God. Remember that we are in the apostasy. Though the creeds of all the great denominations were sound creeds (they differed a little on some points, but on the great basics there was no difference), today the church has been taken over by liberals who totally reject the great doctrines their denominations were founded upon. Folk in these churches have been so brainwashed over the years that though they want to believe they are having their problems. We would do well to be patient with them.

6. *"And others save with fear, pulling them out of the fire"* (verse 23). I do not know whether we'll see a revival in our day or not. We haven't so far. But I do know this, that we can still pull them out of the fire. These are folk whom we would judge to be hopeless sinners. It seems to us that nobody could reach them. I have been amazed at some of the people who have come to the Lord through the medium of radio. People that I have known and, frankly, have given up, have come to Christ by hearing the Word taught on radio. "And others save with fear, pulling them out of the fire!" What a tremendous thing!

A letter has come to me from Fairbanks, Alaska, which illustrates this:

Because KJNP is the loudest voice in the Arctic (50,000 watts) hundreds of bush pilots lock onto the station to guide them into the city of Fairbanks, and they must listen to what is on the air at the time. Just a few weeks ago one of the wicked bush pilots was locked onto KJNP and, behold, you were broadcasting! By the time he reached Fairbanks he had re-

pented and was wonderfully born again by the Spirit of God.
He is now attending a fundamental church and doing well.
Praise God!

There are a few—one here, two there. If we mean business,
we can still see people being saved today.

May I say to you, friend, there is somebody around you
today whom you can pull out of the fire. If there were a
house on fire with somebody inside of it, you would do
your best to get him out. I'm sure you would. But just
think of the people around you today who are on their way
to a lost eternity, and some of them you can reach. I don't
think you can reach them all. I don't recommend you go
out on the street and hand a tract to everybody who comes
along, but I do say there is somebody you can reach. And
the interesting thing is you are the only one who can reach
them—they would never listen to this preacher—but they
will listen to you. They have respect for you. They have
confidence in you. Yet you have never told them about the
Savior who has saved you. That is the type of witnessing we
need in days of apostasy.

7. *"Hating even the garment spotted by the flesh"*
(verse 23). What really is the flesh, as it is used in the Word
of God? I think we have the wrong idea of it today. The
word "flesh" does not necessarily mean only that which is
licentious, although it includes that. The "flesh" refers to
this old nature that we have. And this old nature does not
always go in the direction of licentiousness. There are a
great many people today who are art lovers and music lovers. There are cultured folk who would never rob anyone
or engage in immorality. But without Christ they are lost
people, and they are living in the flesh—as much in the
flesh as any drunkard on Main Street. In God's sight they
are just as lost. God says that "all have sinned, and come
short of the glory of God" (Romans 3:23). *All* come under
that category.

You and I today are to hate the garment that is spotted by the flesh. May I make it personal? *Pride* is of the flesh. *Gossip* is of the flesh. *Harsh criticism* is of the flesh. And there is a lot of the flesh manifested in our churches. This pious pose that many have toward spirituality is of the flesh and not of God at all. Even Paul the apostle, a religious man who was converted to Christ, said, "Oh, wretched man that I am! Who shall deliver me from the body of this death?" (Romans 7:24). This is not a lost man asking for salvation. This is the cry of a saved man who was living in the flesh. Anything that Vernon McGee produces of the flesh God hates, regardless of how religious it is or how pious it might be or how much Bible it has in it. If it is of the flesh He hates it. Only that which the Spirit of God produces through us can He use. We should learn to hate "even the garment spotted by the flesh."

These are the seven things we are to do in days of apostasy.

LET'S GET GOING!

Dwight L. Moody said, "I look upon this world as a wrecked vessel. Its ruin is getting nearer and nearer. God said to me, 'Moody, here's a lifeboat. Go out and rescue as many as you can before the crash comes.' " And up until the ministry of Billy Graham, Moody looked into the faces of more people than any man who ever lived, and he reduced the population of hell by 200,000. My friend, if God could use Moody, He can use you and He can use me in these days of apostasy. Moody said, "I got the lifeboat and went out." What about you, Christian friend, in these days?

I hear so many people complaining today, and these are good days to complain. They say, "Oh, look at the stock market! . . . Oh, look at the riots! . . . Oh, look at what's happening in the world!" Sure, it's all happening. We had better keep our eyes open—lots more things are going to happen. We've seen more things take place recently than we saw in the entire century! And the next several months may be tremendous. But, my friend, I would rather live today and get out the Word of God than to live in any other period in the history of this world!

I say it's thrilling to get out the Word of God in these days of apostasy. These complaining and criticizing Christians—God, have mercy on them in a world that's on fire and a world today that probably is moving toward revolution. But thank God we can still get out the Word of God. Let's be about our Father's business.

—— 14 ——

THE PULPIT AND THE WELL OF LIFE*

(John 12:21)

"The same came to Philip . . . saying, Sir, we would see Jesus." (John 12:21)

On the back of the pulpit of the Church of the Open Door in downtown Los Angeles is placed the well-known scriptural injunction, "Sir, we would see Jesus." This familiar Scripture is found in many pulpits today as a constant and urgent reminder to the preacher of the primary purpose of the pulpit.

After mentioning to the Board of the church that I had seen this Scripture in so many pulpits, they placed it on the pulpit of the Church of the Open Door without any suggestion on my part. This direct imperative is appropriate in an age that has witnessed the reduction of the pulpit to a soapbox for the propagation of a philosophical nostrum, a

---

* Taken from *We Prepare and Preach,* by Clarence Stonelynn Roddy, Ph.D. Copyright 1959, Moody Bible Institute of Chicago. Moody Press. Used by permission.

sideshow barker's platform for any religious racket, and the stage for the entertainment of habitués of church buildings.

There is an added motto which might be placed helpfully alongside the scriptural injunction. It is not scriptural but is very familiar to our contemporary society. The motto is "This Is Your Life."

The pulpit is a mirror held up to the life of the minister, and the life of the minister flows—all unconsciously to him —through the pulpit. Diligent study habits will be reflected from the pulpit; laziness and carelessness become obvious in the glare and searching spotlight of the pulpit. What is in the "well" of his life will come up through the "bucket" of the pulpit. This frightful fact was given to me as a student in seminary, and the experiences of a quarter of a century have corroborated the accuracy of this thesis.

The contemporary pulpit is immeasurably weak. This is not a day of great preachers. The present-day preacher is an organizer, a promoter, a counselor, a youth director, a Christian education expert, a builder, a fundraiser, and a "good fellow" in the community. He does not need to be a man of God, according to modern standards.

In spite of warped and perverted attitudes toward the preacher and the pulpit, there are three objectives that I have attempted to keep in mind in the preparation and delivery of a sermon.

SIMPLICITY IN PREPARATION

There is a pernicious and contagious disease which has recently affected the ministry which can be designated as "neointellectualism." There is a definite aim to make the sermon a masterpiece of erudition. The attempt seems to be to take simple truths and make them complex rather than take profound truths and make them simple. It was said of our Lord Jesus Christ, "And the common people heard him gladly." Even Paul, the intellectual giant, wrote to the Corinthians who boasted of their worldly wisdom:

And I, brethren, when I came to you, came not with excellency of speech or of wisdom, declaring unto you the testimony of God. For I determined not to know anything among you, save Jesus Christ, and him crucified. (1 Corinthians 2:1-2)

It was fortunate for me that during my college days I met a very scholarly minister who had the knack of taking the profound truths of theology and translating them into the simple language of the ordinary person. I asked him for his secret. He assured me that this priceless gift was one that needed to be developed and cultivated. His formula went something like this: In the preparation of the sermon every effort should be made to attain simplicity—then go over the sermon the second time to reduce it to the simplest common denominator. Go over the sermon again and again until you are ashamed of its simplicity, then preach the sermon so that the children can understand it. Afterward, one of the spiritual saints will come up to remark about the depth and profundity of the message. It is difficult to make the message too simple.

The preachers of the past and present who have ministered to the crowds spoke in the language of the common people. The late Dr. Harry A. Ironside, who spoke to thousands each week of his ministry, had two homely expressions which are apropos: Jesus told us to feed His sheep, not His giraffes. Put the cookies on the bottom shelf for the kiddies to get. This method is fully illustrated in the Bible relating to the reading of the Law by Ezra on a pulpit of wood before the Water Gate:

So they read in the book in the law of God distinctly, and gave the sense, and caused them to understand the reading. (Nehemiah 8:8)

SCRIPTURAL IN CONTENT

The old-fashioned methods of preaching were topical, textual, and expository. There is a tendency today to depart from all three—in fact, to depart from Scripture altogether. Sermons have become "pep talks" on psychology, political speeches on the United Nations, or propaganda for some new fad. Someone has defined the modern church as a place where a mild-mannered man gets up before some mild-mannered people and urges them to be more mild-mannered.

The expository sermon is not passé, it is still the only effective method of reaching the hearts of the listeners. An entire passage should be considered in a sermon. The passage should be read and studied until it is mastered, then it should be arranged in a logical division. The sermon should be more than a running commentary on the verses. Painstaking study will reveal a logical division and method of presentation in every passage.

The preacher who uses the Word of God has the Holy Spirit to lead him and to apply the Word to the hearts of his listeners. A preacher who departs from Scripture in his preaching robs himself of his greatest assistance. The Word of God is still "the sword of the Spirit." Likewise, the Holy Spirit will give him added insight:

> *But as it is written, Eye hath not seen, nor ear heard, neither have entered into the heart of man, the things which God hath prepared for them that love him. But God hath revealed them unto us by his Spirit: for the Spirit searcheth all things, yea, the deep things of God.*
> (1 Corinthians 2:9–10)

Furthermore, God has promised to bless *His Word* and not the pet theories of the preacher:

> *So shall my word be that goeth forth out of my mouth: it shall not return unto me void, but it shall accomplish*

that which I please, and it shall prosper in the thing whereto I sent it. (Isaiah 55:11)

Sermon content is far more important than preparation and delivery. The man who is filled with the Word of God will find a way of giving it forth:

And if I say, I will not make mention of him, nor speak any more in his name, then there is in my heart as it were a burning fire shut up in my bones, and I am weary with forbearing, and I cannot contain. (Jeremiah 20:9, ASV)

SINCERITY OF EXPRESSION

There is a grave danger of the preacher's becoming professional in the pulpit. He can easily become an actor who is merely playing a part. The theoretical and academic are to be studiously avoided. He should not major in that which he has not himself experienced. Certain doctrines may become an obsession rather than the practice of the preacher. The head so easily runs faster than the heart.

Unfortunately, there are men in the ministry who are sincere, but their voice ministers against them. There are others who have a sincere voice but are engaged in a religious racket. This is especially true of the radio. Spiritually minded Christians will eventually make the distinction. All of this should not preclude the minister from being sincere in his own ministry.

Three messages must be prepared a week by the average preacher; and preach he must, whether he likes it or not. Therefore, he should seek a burning heart in prayer before God. He should speak as Wesley said: "A dying man to dying men!" McCheyne wrote, "Speak for eternity." Paul stated it in the language of the Spirit: "Woe unto me if I preach not the gospel." The prophet Jeremiah cried that the Word was a fire shut up in his bones.

The preacher who does not love to preach should carefully examine his call to the ministry. It should be the burden of his soul. The Lord Jesus Christ could report to the Father, "I have given them thy word!" I trust that this statement can be put in your final report and in mine.